WALKTHROUGH OF DYNASTY WARRIORS: ORIGINS

Unlock every battle, character and weapon

Marie J Smith

Table of contents

Introduction to Dynasty Warriors: Origins   5
    Storyline and Historical Context   6
    Key Features and Innovations   8
    Platforms and Release Information   10

Chapter 2: Getting Started   13
    Game Installation and Setup   13
    Controls and Gameplay Mechanics   20
    Selecting Your Protagonist and Companions   24

Chapter 3:Gameplay Mechanics   28
    Utilizing Tactics and Grand Tactics   37
    Understanding Morale and Fortitude   42
    Navigating the World Map and Battlefields   46

Chapter 4:. Walkthrough: Main Campaign   51
    Chapter 2: The Rise of Warlords   55
    Chapter 3: The Battle of Hulao Gate   58
    Chapter 4: The Formation of Alliances   62
    Chapter 5: The Battle of Chibi   66
    Decision Points and Multiple Endings   70

Chapter 5 Characters and Companions   75
    Overview of Playable Characters   75
    Companion Abilities and Roles   79
    Unlocking Additional Characters   88

Chapter 6:Weapons and Equipment   93
    Traits and Customization Options   98
    Purchasing and Finding Rare Weapons   103

Equipment Strategies for Different Battles	108
Chapter 7. Side Missions and Activities	**114**
Missions: Objectives and Rewards	114
Skirmishes: Challenges and Strategies	118
Visiting Towns and Interacting with NPCs	123
Unlockable Content and Secrets	128
Chapter 8: Tips and Strategies	**134**
Combat Tips for Beginners and Advanced Players	134
Effective Use of Tactics and Companions	139
Managing Resources and Upgrades	145

All rights reserved, no part of this publication may be reproduced, distributed in any form or by any means including photocopying, recording, electronic or mechanical methods without the prior written permission of the publisher except in the case of brief quotations embodied in critical reviews and certain other non commercial uses permitted by copyright law

Copyright © Marie J Smith 2024

Introduction to Dynasty Warriors: Origins

Overview of the Game

Dynasty Warriors: Origins redefines the beloved hack-and-slash franchise by going back to its roots and exploring the rich tapestry of the Three Kingdoms saga with unmatched depth. This game is not just another addition to the Dynasty Warriors series—it is a bold reimagining that blends cinematic storytelling, tactical depth, and the signature action that fans adore.

At its core, Origins retains the exhilarating gameplay the franchise is known for, where players charge into massive battles, taking on hordes of enemies and commanding armies in real-time combat. However, this title goes a step further by introducing enhanced AI, dynamic environments, and a more nuanced approach to warfare. The new Dynamic Battlefield System ensures that no two battles feel the same, as weather, terrain, and morale shifts play a crucial role in determining the outcome.

The game introduces a host of new features, including an intricate character development system, interactive cutscenes, and multiple story paths. Players will experience the drama of ancient China not just as passive observers but as active participants. The decision-making mechanic ensures that your actions on the battlefield and during dialogues shape the course of history, adding layers of replayability.

Moreover, Dynasty Warriors: Origins caters to both veterans and newcomers with its scalable difficulty, robust tutorials, and accessible gameplay mechanics. Whether you are here for nostalgia or looking for a modern entry point into the franchise, Origins promises a rich and fulfilling experience that honors its legacy while charting a new path forward.

Storyline and Historical Context

Set during the waning days of the Han Dynasty, Dynasty Warriors: Origins immerses players in one of the most tumultuous periods of Chinese history. The empire, once a beacon of stability and prosperity, is now plagued by corruption, rebellion, and power struggles. Against this backdrop, the game introduces legendary figures such as Liu Bei, Cao Cao, and Sun Jian, whose ambitions will shape the future of China.

The narrative begins with the Yellow Turban Rebellion, an uprising led by Zhang Jiao and his brothers. What starts as a movement born out of desperation soon spirals into a nationwide crisis, forcing the imperial court to rely on regional warlords to suppress the chaos. Players are thrust into these battles, experiencing the conflict from multiple perspectives.

As the story progresses, players witness the fall of the Han Dynasty and the emergence of three powerful kingdoms: Wei, Wu, and Shu. Each faction is portrayed with depth, exploring the ideals, alliances, and betrayals that define their leaders. From the coalition against the tyrant Dong Zhuo to the pivotal Battle of Red Cliffs, the game takes players through iconic moments of the Three Kingdoms era, reimagined with dramatic flair.

What sets Dynasty Warriors: Origins apart is its commitment to historical authenticity paired with creative storytelling. Detailed recreations of ancient Chinese architecture, attire, and landscapes transport players back in time, while the characters' personal struggles add emotional weight to the epic battles. The game not only educates players about the era but also inspires them to delve deeper into its rich history.

Key Features and Innovations

Dynasty Warriors: Origins boasts a plethora of features that make it a standout title in the franchise:

1. Dynamic Battlefield System

The Dynamic Battlefield System introduces real-time environmental changes that affect combat strategy. Sudden rain can dampen fire-based attacks, while muddy terrain slows troop movements, forcing players to adapt their tactics. These changes create a living, breathing battlefield where awareness and quick thinking are key.

2. Enhanced Character Development

Unlike previous titles, Origins allows for deeper character customization. Players can unlock unique abilities, weapons, and combos through an expansive skill tree. Each character also has a moral alignment system that evolves based on decisions made during missions, affecting their relationships and story outcomes.

3. Branching Storylines and Replayability

Player choices have a tangible impact on the game's narrative. Align with different factions, forge unlikely alliances, or betray trusted allies—your decisions shape the story and unlock multiple endings. This feature ensures that every playthrough offers a unique experience.

4. Next-Generation Graphics and Sound

The game harnesses the power of modern consoles to deliver breathtaking visuals, from intricately designed character models to sprawling battlefields teeming with life. The soundtrack combines traditional Chinese instruments with orchestral compositions, adding to the immersive atmosphere.

5. Co-op and Multiplayer Modes
For the first time, players can team up with friends in cooperative missions or engage in competitive multiplayer battles. These modes emphasize strategy and coordination, adding a new layer of excitement to the franchise's gameplay.

Platforms and Release Information

On PlayStation 5 and Xbox Series X/S, the game takes full advantage of advanced hardware capabilities. With ray-traced lighting, ultra-high-definition textures, and a buttery-smooth 60 FPS performance mode, Dynasty Warriors: Origins showcases the potential of next-gen consoles. These versions also feature faster load times, ensuring seamless transitions between cutscenes, menus, and battles. The PC version is equally impressive, offering customizable graphics settings to cater to a wide spectrum of hardware configurations, from high-end rigs to mid-tier gaming setups.

The Nintendo Switch version brings the franchise to handheld enthusiasts, ensuring fans can take the action with them on the go. While it sacrifices some visual fidelity to maintain a stable frame rate, this version offers all the core features and gameplay mechanics present on other platforms. Players can enjoy the same dynamic combat, branching narratives, and expansive campaigns, making it a commendable option for portable gaming.

Beyond technical specifications, the release of Dynasty Warriors: Origins was accompanied by a robust lineup of content. The standard edition includes the full base game, while the deluxe edition offers additional character skins, exclusive weapons, and a digital artbook and soundtrack. For collectors, a limited-edition physical release includes a steelbook case, a map of ancient China, and a miniature replica of an iconic weapon from the game.

Post-launch support has also been a major focus for the developers. Regular updates bring quality-of-life improvements, balancing tweaks, and new free content, such as side missions and playable characters. A comprehensive DLC roadmap promises expansions that delve into untold stories of the Three Kingdoms era, introducing fresh challenges and gameplay mechanics to keep the experience engaging for months to come.

Dynasty Warriors: Origins has been celebrated for its commitment to fans and its thoughtful innovations. Whether you're playing on a high-performance console, a gaming PC, or a handheld device, this game promises an unforgettable journey through the legendary world of the Three Kingdoms. With a blend of accessibility, technical excellence, and rich storytelling, it sets a new standard for the series, ensuring its place in the pantheon of great action games.

Chapter 2: Getting Started

Game Installation and Setup

Before embarking on your journey through ancient China in Dynasty Warriors: Origins, it's essential to ensure the game is installed and set up correctly for an optimal experience. This subchapter will guide you through the process step by step, helping you get everything ready, whether you're playing on a console or PC.

1. Platform-Specific Installation

PlayStation 5 and Xbox Series X/S: Start by inserting the game disc (if using a physical copy) or downloading the game from your console's digital store. For digital versions, ensure your console has sufficient storage space, as Dynasty Warriors: Origins requires approximately 50 GB. Once downloaded, the system will automatically install the game. Players are encouraged to check for updates, as a day-one patch often resolves initial bugs or adds features.

PC Installation:
For PC users, the game is available on platforms such as Steam and the Epic Games Store. After purchasing,

download the game through the respective launcher. Verify your PC meets the minimum system requirements, which include at least an Intel Core i5 processor, 8 GB RAM, and an NVIDIA GTX 970 graphics card. Higher settings will require more robust hardware for 60 FPS gameplay. Once downloaded, launch the game to complete any required initial setup.

Nintendo Switch:
Insert the cartridge for physical editions or download the game through the Nintendo eShop. The Switch version requires approximately 15 GB of free space, so ensure your system storage or microSD card has adequate capacity. For portable players, using a pro controller can enhance the experience.

2. Initial Setup

Language and Region Settings:
Upon launching the game for the first time, you'll be prompted to select your preferred language and subtitle options. The game supports a wide array of languages for both text and voice overs, ensuring players worldwide can immerse themselves fully.

Audio and Graphics Optimization:
Adjust the audio levels for music, sound effects, and dialogue to suit your preferences. On consoles, settings

are straightforward, while PC players can fine-tune graphical options such as resolution, anti-aliasing, and texture quality for optimal performance.

3. Account and Save Data

Creating a Save File:
Ensure you have storage available for creating save files. Cloud saving options are supported on all platforms, offering a seamless way to transfer progress across devices or safeguard your gameplay data.

Online Features:
For those interested in multiplayer or co-op modes, linking your platform account (e.g., PlayStation Network, Xbox Live, or Steam) is essential. This also unlocks access to leaderboards, achievements, and downloadable content (DLC).

By following these steps, you'll ensure a smooth start to your journey in Dynasty Warriors: Origins. Ready your equipment and prepare for the adventure of a lifetime!

User Interface Overview

The user interface (UI) in Dynasty Warriors: Origins has been designed to be both visually appealing and highly functional, ensuring players can focus on the action without feeling overwhelmed. Understanding the various elements of the UI is crucial for navigating battles, managing your character, and strategizing effectively. This subchapter provides a detailed breakdown of the interface, highlighting its key features and how to use them effectively.

1. Main Menu Overview
Upon launching the game, players are greeted by the main menu, which serves as the central hub for accessing all major features. The following options are prominently displayed:

Story Mode: Dive into the main campaign and experience the epic saga of the Three Kingdoms.
Free Mode: Replay battles from the campaign with any unlocked character or set your preferred conditions.
Multiplayer: Access online co-op or competitive modes.
Settings: Adjust audio, graphics, and gameplay preferences.
Extras: View collectibles, achievements, and gallery items, including cutscenes and artwork.
The menu's clean design and intuitive navigation make it easy for players to jump straight into the action or fine-tune their settings.

2. In-Game HUD (Heads-Up Display)

The in-game HUD is your window into the battlefield. Here's a breakdown of its components:

Health and Stamina Bars:
  Located at the top-left corner of the screen, the health bar (red) shows your character's vitality, while the stamina bar (yellow or blue) tracks your ability to execute special moves and dashes.

Mini-Map:
Positioned in the top-right corner, the mini-map is essential for situational awareness. It highlights enemy and ally positions, key objectives, and points of interest, such as supply depots or command posts.

Mission Objectives:
Displayed in the top-center portion of the screen, these provide real-time updates on your current goals, such as defeating a specific enemy officer or capturing a strategic point.

Action Prompts:
Near the bottom of the screen, context-sensitive prompts guide players on actions like interacting with objects, executing finishers, or triggering story events.

Skill and Special Ability Indicators:

Below the health bar, icons represent your equipped skills or special abilities. Cooldowns or resource requirements are clearly displayed, allowing you to strategize their use.

3. Menus and Submenus

During gameplay, the pause menu provides access to additional options:

Character Management: View and equip weapons, armor, and accessories. The skill tree is also accessible here, allowing you to unlock or upgrade abilities.
Battlefield Overview: A detailed map with tactical information, including the status of allied forces and enemy strongholds.
Options: Adjust gameplay settings or toggle UI elements to customize your experience.

4. Accessibility Features
The game includes a variety of accessibility options to ensure inclusivity. Players can resize text, adjust color contrasts, enable subtitles for all dialogue, and toggle simplified controls for those with limited mobility.

Mastering the user interface is the first step toward commanding the battlefield with confidence. Familiarize yourself with these elements, and you'll be well-prepared to handle any challenge that comes your way.

Controls and Gameplay Mechanics

One of the hallmarks of Dynasty Warriors: Origins is its smooth and intuitive control system, designed to make the epic battles of the Three Kingdoms both accessible and deeply engaging. This subchapter delves into the controls across various platforms and introduces the core gameplay mechanics that define the Dynasty Warriors experience.

1. Platform-Specific Controls

Console (PlayStation and Xbox):
On consoles, the controls utilize the standard button layout for action games:

Movement: Use the left analog stick to navigate your character and the right analog stick to control the camera.
Basic Attacks: Light attacks are mapped to Square/X, while heavy attacks are performed with Triangle/Y.
Special Abilities: Press R1/RB to trigger character-specific special moves, consuming stamina or a special meter.

Jump and Dash: X/A allows your character to jump, while pressing L3 initiates a dash to evade enemy strikes or close the distance.

Target Lock: L2/LT locks onto a specific enemy, ensuring precision during intense battles.

PC (Keyboard and Mouse):
PC players can opt for a keyboard-and-mouse setup or a controller for a familiar experience. Default keybindings include:

WASD for movement and the mouse for camera control.
Left-click for light attacks and right-click for heavy attacks.
E for interacting with objects or triggering context-sensitive actions.

Q and Shift for dashing or activating abilities.

Customization options allow players to remap keys to suit their preferences.

Nintendo Switch:
On the Switch, controls are optimized for portability and Joy-Con usage. Button mapping remains similar to other consoles, though motion controls can be enabled for precision targeting in certain game modes.

2. Core Gameplay Mechanics

Attack Combos:
Combining light and heavy attacks allows for devastating combos, unique to each character. Experimenting with different sequences unlocks hidden moves and creates opportunities to overwhelm enemies.

Musou Gauge and Ultimate Attacks:
The iconic Musou system returns, enabling players to unleash powerful area-of-effect attacks when the gauge is full. Build the Musou meter by landing hits and taking damage, then trigger your ultimate attack to turn the tide of battle.

Skill Trees and Customization:
Characters can be customized through skill trees, allowing players to unlock passive bonuses, new attacks, and enhanced abilities. This system encourages strategic planning and ensures no two warriors feel the same.

Morale System:
The morale of your allies and enemies impacts their performance on the battlefield. High morale boosts attack power and survivability, while low morale can lead to defections or retreats. Players can influence morale by completing objectives, defeating enemy officers, and capturing strongholds.

Interactive Environments:
The Dynamic Battlefield System introduces destructible environments and terrain-based strategies. For example, players can collapse a bridge to block reinforcements or use fire attacks to devastate enemy camps.

Commanding Troops:
As a leader, you'll issue commands to allied units, directing them to defend positions, attack specific targets, or regroup. The command wheel, accessible via R2/RT or a dedicated key, streamlines this process.

3. Mastering the Learning Curve

The game includes a comprehensive tutorial mode to introduce players to these mechanics gradually. Early missions are designed to teach fundamental skills, while optional challenges help refine advanced techniques. Whether you're a novice or a seasoned player, Dynasty Warriors: Origins ensures you're equipped to conquer the battlefield.

By understanding the controls and mechanics, players gain the tools needed to thrive in Dynasty Warriors: Origins. Success lies not just in mastering the art of combat but also in making strategic choices that shape the fate of the Three Kingdoms.

Selecting Your Protagonist and Companions

One of the most exciting aspects of Dynasty Warriors: Origins is the ability to choose your protagonist and assemble a team of loyal companions. This system not only personalizes your journey through the Three Kingdoms but also influences the storyline, combat style, and overall gameplay experience. In this subchapter, we'll explore the process of character selection, the role of companions, and how to maximize their potential on the battlefield.

1. Choosing Your Protagonist

At the start of the game, players are presented with a roster of legendary warriors, each hailing from one of the Three Kingdoms: Wei, Wu, or Shu. While your initial choice doesn't lock you into a specific faction, it sets the tone for your campaign, as every character has unique motivations, abilities, and story arcs.

Faction Leaders:
Players can opt to play as iconic leaders such as Cao Cao (Wei), Liu Bei (Shu), or Sun Jian (Wu). These characters offer campaigns that focus on large-scale strategies and leadership challenges, ideal for players who enjoy a mix of diplomacy and combat.
Rising Stars:

Characters like Zhao Yun, Xiahou Dun, and Sun Ce represent younger warriors whose arcs focus on loyalty, ambition, and personal growth. Choosing these characters allows for a more action-driven experience with personal stakes.

Custom Character (Optional):
For players seeking a unique experience, *Dynasty Warriors: Origins offers a robust character creation system. You can design a custom hero, selecting everything from their appearance to their weapon style and allegiance. This feature adds a layer of replayability, as your custom character's presence can alter the dynamics of the main story.

2. Recruiting Companions
Throughout the campaign, you'll encounter numerous officers and allies who can join your cause. The recruitment system is dynamic, with each companion offering distinct skills and benefits. Companions are not just AI-controlled allies; their presence can significantly impact your strategy and the unfolding narrative.

Types of Companions:
Combat Specialists: Focused on offensive or defensive roles, these companions excel at handling specific battlefield challenges.

Support Units: Healers, strategists, and morale boosters who enhance your overall effectiveness in prolonged battles.

Story-Driven Characters: These individuals come with unique storylines and missions, adding depth to your campaign and unlocking exclusive rewards.

Building Relationships:
Companions are more than just tools for combat—they are integral to the game's emotional depth. Engaging in conversations, completing personal quests, and making choices that align with their values will strengthen your bond. High affinity levels unlock powerful combo attacks, strategic advantages, and exclusive story content.

3. Balancing Your Team
Success in Dynasty Warriors: Origins often hinges on assembling a balanced team. While it's tempting to rely solely on powerhouse warriors, a mix of offensive, defensive, and support-oriented companions ensures you're prepared for any scenario. For example:

Pairing a tanky fighter with a nimble archer and a healer provides versatility on the battlefield.

Deploying companions with siege skills can turn the tide during fortress assaults.

Assigning a strategist to monitor troop movements can prevent ambushes and maximize your efficiency.

4. Impact on the Narrative
The characters you choose to travel with influence the progression of the story. Certain allies may trigger exclusive missions, offer unique insights into key events, or even shift the balance of power within the Three Kingdoms. Building relationships carefully and choosing companions that align with your goals can open up new paths in the campaign and lead to multiple endings.

By thoughtfully selecting your protagonist and companions, you'll create a dynamic and personalized journey through the epic saga of Dynasty Warriors: Origins. Each choice brings its own challenges and rewards, ensuring no two playthroughs are ever the same.

Chapter 3: Gameplay Mechanics

Combat System: Attacks, Parries, and Arts

The combat system in Dynasty Warriors: Origins builds on the franchise's legacy of fast-paced, hack-and-slash gameplay, while incorporating refined mechanics that add depth and strategy. Whether you're mowing down hordes of enemies or engaging in intense one-on-one duels, mastering the combat system is essential for success. This subchapter provides a detailed breakdown of attacks, parries, and the powerful character-specific arts that define the game's action.

1. Basic and Advanced Attacks

The foundation of combat lies in your ability to execute light and heavy attacks. While light attacks are quick and effective for dispatching minor enemies, heavy attacks deliver devastating blows that can stagger or break the defenses of tougher opponents.

Light Attacks:
Light attacks are performed with Square/X (consoles) or left-click (PC). These attacks are fast and chainable into combos, making them ideal for crowd control. However,

they deal less damage and are less effective against heavily armored foes.

Heavy Attacks:
Heavy attacks are executed with Triangle/Y (consoles) or right-click (PC). These moves deal higher damage and often have additional effects, such as launching enemies into the air or breaking shields. Combining light and heavy attacks unlocks advanced combo sequences unique to each character.

Aerial Attacks:
Jumping and attacking mid-air allows for creative combat strategies, especially against enemies in elevated positions or during mounted combat.

2. Parries and Counters
The parry mechanic introduces a layer of defensive strategy to combat. By timing your block perfectly against an enemy's attack, you can stagger them and open up opportunities for devastating counterattacks.

Parrying:
Press L1/LB (console) or Shift (PC) just before an enemy attack lands to parry. Success requires precise timing, but it leaves opponents vulnerable for a brief moment.

Counters:
After a successful parry, pressing a heavy attack triggers a counter move. These counters are character-specific and can deal massive damage or trigger special effects, such as disarming opponents or creating area knockbacks.

Blocking:
Holding L1/LB (console) or Shift (PC) blocks incoming attacks, reducing damage but draining stamina. Blocking is essential when overwhelmed by multiple enemies, but it's not infallible against strong or unblockable moves.

3. Character Arts and Special Abilities
Each character possesses unique abilities, known as Arts, that set them apart on the battlefield. These are tied to the new "Energy Gauge," which fills as you attack and defend during combat.

Basic Arts:
These are low-energy abilities that enhance combat flow. For example, a quick dash attack to close distances or a small AoE (area of effect) strike to control crowds.

Signature Arts:
Each character has a signature move that highlights their combat style and personality. For instance, Zhao Yun's Spear Storm sweeps enemies in a wide arc, while Cao

28

Cao's Tactical Strike summons reinforcements to bolster your morale.

Ultimate Arts: When the Energy Gauge is full, unleash your character's Ultimate Art—a cinematic and devastating attack that can shift the tide of battle. These moves are best saved for bosses or overwhelming situations.

4. Environmental Interactions

The battlefield itself becomes a weapon in *Dynasty Warriors: Origins. By engaging with the environment, players can gain strategic advantages.

Destructible Objects:
Destroy barrels or carts for bonus items, such as health potions or temporary buffs.

Interactive Elements:
Certain maps include traps like collapsible bridges or flaming barricades. Use these to your advantage by luring enemies into hazardous zones.

5. Stamina Management

Combat in Dynasty Warriors: Origins introduces a stamina bar, which governs actions like dashing, parrying, and performing certain Arts. Balancing stamina use is critical, as depleting it leaves you vulnerable and unable to block or perform advanced moves.

Weapon Types and Their Advantages

In Dynasty Warriors: Origins, the wide variety of weapon types available ensures that every player can find a fighting style that suits their preferences. From swift and agile swords to massive, crowd-controlling polearms, each weapon type comes with unique advantages, disadvantages, and tactical uses. This subchapter explores the weapon types in detail, helping players understand their strengths and the best scenarios to use them.

1. Weapon Categories

The game features a diverse selection of weapons, each falling into one of the following categories:

Swords and Dual Blades:
Advantages: Balanced in speed, power, and versatility, swords and dual blades are ideal for beginners. They allow for fluid combos and quick evasion, making them suitable for most combat situations.
Notable Users: Liu Bei's curved blade focuses on precision, while Sun Ce's dual blades deliver rapid strikes that overwhelm enemies. Best Use: Excellent for one-on-one duels and engaging mid-sized groups.

Polearms and Spears:

Advantages: These weapons offer superior range and sweeping attacks, making them effective for controlling large crowds. They also excel in mounted combat, providing reach and power.
Notable Users: Zhao Yun's spear strikes a balance between speed and power, while Zhang Liao's halberd is a devastating weapon for crowd control.
Best Use: Ideal for breaking through enemy lines and handling hordes.

Great Axes and Hammers:
Advantages: Unparalleled in raw power, these heavy weapons deal massive damage with every swing. They can break shields and stagger enemies but are slower than other weapon types.
Notable Users: Xu Huang wields a massive great axe that can crush defenses, while Dian Wei's hammer smashes through enemy ranks.
Best Use: Perfect for targeting heavily armored foes or clearing tightly packed groups.

Bows and Crossbows:
Advantages: Ranged weapons provide a safe way to deal damage from a distance. They're particularly effective for picking off enemy officers or weakening foes before engaging them in melee.

Notable Users: Huang Zhong's longbow delivers precision strikes, while Sun Shangxiang's dual crossbows offer rapid fire for sustained ranged damage.
Best Use: Best suited for support roles, harassing enemies, or targeting vulnerable opponents.

Exotic Weapons:
Advantages: These weapons, such as fans, whips, or chakrams, provide unique attack patterns and elemental effects. They often require a higher skill level but reward players with versatility and flair.
Notable Users: Zhuge Liang's war fan creates whirlwinds, and Diao Chan's whip combines grace and lethality.
Best Use: Excellent for players who enjoy creative and unorthodox combat styles.

2. Weapon Customization
Weapons in Dynasty Warriors: Origins can be upgraded and enhanced to fit your playstyle:
Elemental Infusions: Add fire, lightning, or ice elements to your weapons for additional effects. For example, fire deals damage over time, while ice slows enemies.
Stat Boosts: Attach runes to improve attack power, defense, or speed.
Special Traits: Unlock unique weapon traits, such as lifesteal or critical hit bonuses, by completing challenges or progressing through the campaign.

3. Weapon Synergies

Equipping weapons that complement your companions' loadouts can create powerful synergies:

Offensive Pairings: Combine a ranged companion with a melee weapon user to balance attack range.

Tactical Combos: Use a heavy weapon to break enemy defenses, then switch to a faster weapon for rapid follow-ups.

4. Adapting to the Battlefield

Each battlefield presents unique challenges, and selecting the right weapon can be the difference between victory and defeat:

In tight quarters, fast weapons like swords or dual blades excel at keeping you mobile.

On open plains, spears and polearms shine for their ability to hit multiple enemies at range.

During sieges, ranged weapons like bows are invaluable for picking off defenders from a distance.

Utilizing Tactics and Grand Tactics

In Dynasty Warriors: Origins, success on the battlefield depends not only on raw combat prowess but also on the effective use of tactics and grand strategies. The game emphasizes strategic decision-making, encouraging players to think beyond simple attacks and utilize the tools at their disposal to turn the tide of battle. This subchapter explores the tactical mechanics in detail, from basic strategies to overarching grand tactics.

1. Tactical Elements on the Battlefield
Troop Commands:
As a leader, you can issue orders to your allies in real-time. Using the command wheel (accessible via R2/RT or a designated key), you can direct troops to:
Defend key locations.
Launch coordinated attacks on enemy strongholds.
Regroup and provide support in high-pressure situations.

Delegating tasks to your troops allows you to focus on high-value targets while ensuring the overall success of your army.

Objective Prioritization:
Each battle is broken into primary and secondary objectives. Completing secondary objectives, such as rescuing allies or capturing outposts, often grants bonuses like increased morale, reinforcements, or special items. Strategic players should balance completing these objectives while pursuing the main goal.

Environmental Tactics: The Dynamic Battlefield System introduces terrain-based strategies. For example:

Use high ground to gain an advantage in ranged combat. Lure enemies into narrow choke points to minimize their numbers.

Exploit destructible elements like barricades and bridges to disrupt enemy movements.

2. Special Battlefield Tactics

Ambushes and Flanking:

Surprise attacks can devastate enemy formations and lower their morale. Use the mini-map to identify potential ambush points, such as forests or hidden pathways. Coordinating with companions to execute flanking maneuvers ensures maximum impact.

Siege Tactics:

During castle or fort battles, siege tactics become essential. Utilize battering rams to break gates, deploy ladders to scale walls, and destroy enemy artillery to secure an advantage. Timing and coordination are critical to prevent heavy losses during sieges.

Defensive Strategies: In missions where you must protect a location, focus on fortifying chokepoints, healing allies, and setting traps. Defensive tactics prioritize survival and maintaining control over strategic zones.

3. Grand Tactics System

Dynasty Warriors: Origins introduces the Grand Tactics System, a feature that allows players to enact overarching strategies that influence the course of an entire battle:

Morale Boosters: Spending morale points gained from successful skirmishes can unlock temporary boosts for your army, such as increased attack power, faster movement, or improved defense.

Reinforcement Deployment: Summon reinforcements to critical locations on the battlefield. This feature is particularly useful for defending outposts or launching surprise counterattacks.

Weather Manipulation:
Certain battles allow players to influence weather conditions, such as summoning a storm to hinder enemy archers or using fire attacks during dry weather to create widespread chaos.

Strategic Partnerships: Forge alliances with neutral factions or NPCs to gain additional support. These partnerships can be leveraged to weaken stronger enemies or bolster your forces.

4. Balancing Aggression and Strategy

While the game encourages dynamic combat, reckless aggression can lead to failure. Tactical players who carefully assess the battlefield, adjust to changing conditions, and utilize their resources effectively are rewarded with smoother victories and fewer casualties.

Adaptive Playstyle: Watch for shifts in enemy behavior and adjust your strategy accordingly. For example, if enemy morale surges, it may be wise to focus on eliminating their officers to destabilize their forces.

Using Companions Strategically: Assigning companions to specific roles—such as guarding objectives or leading assault teams—adds another layer of strategy to the game. Each companion's unique abilities can complement your overarching plans.

Understanding Morale and Fortitude

Morale and fortitude are critical gameplay elements in Dynasty Warriors: Origins that influence both the flow of battle and the overall outcome of missions. These mechanics add depth to the gameplay, encouraging players to focus on more than just defeating enemies. By understanding and manipulating morale and fortitude, you can tip the scales in your favor, even in the most challenging encounters.

1. What is Morale?

Morale represents the confidence and fighting spirit of your troops and those of the enemy. High morale boosts the combat effectiveness of your forces, making them more resilient and aggressive. Conversely, low morale can lead to weakened attacks, disorganized formations, and even retreat.

Indicators of Morale:

Morale levels are displayed on the battlefield map as colored bars or symbols near unit groups. Green indicates high morale, yellow signifies moderate morale, and red warns of low morale.

How Morale Impacts Combat:

Troops with high morale deal increased damage and are less likely to flee under pressure.

Low morale reduces troop effectiveness and makes them more susceptible to devastating enemy attacks.

Enemy officers with low morale can be defeated more easily, as their troops are less likely to protect them aggressively.

2. Factors Influencing Morale

Several factors can increase or decrease morale during battle:

Positive Influences: Defeating Enemy Officers: Taking down a high-ranking officer significantly lowers enemy morale and inspires your troops.

Capturing Strategic Points**: Securing bases, supply depots, and strongholds boosts allied morale while diminishing enemy confidence.

Completing Objectives: Success in side missions or primary tasks directly raises morale.

Negative Influences:
Losing Key Allies: The death or incapacitation of a companion or allied officer can dramatically lower morale.

Heavy Casualties: Sustaining significant losses weakens the resolve of your forces.

Enemy Reinforcements: The arrival of additional enemy troops can demoralize your side.

3. What is Fortitude?
Fortitude is a secondary mechanic tied to the strength of defensive positions and strategic zones. It reflects how resistant these areas are to enemy attacks and how long they can withstand sieges. High fortitude means a base or stronghold can endure prolonged assaults, while low fortitude makes it vulnerable.

Indicators of Fortitude:

Fortitude levels are displayed on the battlefield map as shields or numerical values near bases.

Fortitude in Combat:
A high-fortitude base requires a concentrated effort to capture, often involving multiple waves of attacks.
Weakening fortitude involves targeting key points such as supply depots or eliminating defending officers.

4. Enhancing Morale and Fortitude
Players can actively bolster their forces' morale and fortitude through strategic actions:

Supporting Allies: Assist struggling allies by joining their fights or completing their objectives. This not only boosts their morale but also stabilizes your lines.
Deploying Reinforcements: Use the Grand Tactics System to summon fresh troops, which can revitalize morale and fortify weak points.
Resource Management: Securing supply lines and maintaining control over resource points ensures steady morale and increases fortitude for defensive positions.

5. Exploiting Enemy Weaknesses
Understanding morale and fortitude is also about identifying and exploiting enemy vulnerabilities:

Target bases with low fortitude to disrupt enemy supply chains and weaken their overall resistance.

Focus on demoralized groups to rout them quickly, creating chaos in enemy ranks.

Use psychological warfare by targeting key enemy officers, causing panic and confusion among their troops.

6. Strategic Importance

Managing morale and fortitude effectively can mean the difference between victory and defeat. These mechanics encourage a balanced playstyle that values strategic decision-making alongside combat prowess. Players who prioritize boosting their forces' morale and fortitude while disrupting the enemy's will find themselves at a significant advantage in every battle.

Navigating the World Map and Battlefields

In Dynasty Warriors: Origins, the world map and battlefield layouts are central to your success. They are not only tools for navigation but also hubs for strategic planning and mission execution. Understanding how to interpret and use these maps effectively will ensure you remain one step ahead of your enemies. This subchapter delves into the design, functionality, and tactical significance of the world map and battlefields.

1. The World Map: Your Strategic Overview
The world map serves as your gateway to missions, resources, and key locations within the Three Kingdoms. It is a dynamic representation of the political and military landscape, constantly evolving based on your progress and decisions.

Key Features:
Faction Territories: Highlighted regions show which areas are controlled by Wei, Wu, Shu, or neutral factions. Borders shift as you win battles or lose territory.
Mission Locations: Active missions are marked with icons, categorized by story objectives, side quests, and optional skirmishes.
Resource Nodes: Locate resource-rich areas such as farms, mines, and trading hubs that boost your army's supplies and morale when controlled.
Special Events*: Temporary events, such as surprise attacks or diplomatic opportunities, are marked with unique symbols.

Planning Your Strategy:
The world map allows you to choose your next move, prioritizing either advancing the storyline or fortifying your position. For example:
Engage in side missions to gather resources before tackling major battles.

Cut off enemy supply lines by capturing territories that produce vital resources.

2. Battlefield Maps: A Tactical Advantage
Each mission takes place on a unique battlefield, ranging from dense forests and sprawling plains to fortified castles and treacherous mountain passes. The battlefield map, accessible during gameplay, provides crucial information about the layout and objectives.

Understanding the Map Layout: Strongholds: Key points of control on the map. Capturing these can shift the tide of battle by spawning reinforcements or granting morale boosts.
Paths and Choke Points: Highlighted routes and narrow passages where ambushes or defenses are most effective.
Enemy and Ally Positions: Real-time indicators show the locations of friendly units and enemy forces, helping you plan your movements.

Interactive Features:
Battlefield maps are not static. Dynamic elements such as weather changes, destructible barriers, and moving reinforcements are reflected in real-time, ensuring you stay informed.

3. Moving Across the World Map and Battlefield

World Map Navigation: On the world map, you can move your forces between regions using a travel system. This may involve marching armies, using waterways, or fast-traveling to friendly locations.

Decisions made during travel—such as choosing to take a risky shortcut or waiting for reinforcements—can have long-term consequences.

Battlefield Movement:
Use the mini-map for immediate navigation during battles. It highlights your position, mission objectives, and nearby threats. Mounts, such as horses, are invaluable for crossing large maps quickly, especially when racing to assist allies or intercept enemy forces.

4. Tactical Use of Maps
Pre-Battle Planning: Before each mission, you can study the battlefield layout and assign roles to your companions. For instance, stationing a defensive ally at a choke point while leading an assault elsewhere can save resources and time.

Mid-Battle Adjustments: Use the battlefield map to monitor troop movements and adjust your strategy dynamically. Spotting a gap in enemy defenses or noticing reinforcements arriving can inform split-second decisions.

Post-Battle Analysis: After each battle, review the map to see which territories have been gained or lost. This helps in planning your next steps on the world map.

5. Map Integration with Game Mechanics

The interplay between the world map and battlefield maps creates a seamless experience where your strategic choices impact every aspect of gameplay. For example:

Controlling more regions on the world map provides better resources for your army, which translates to stronger performance in battles.

Losing a critical stronghold on a battlefield may weaken your faction's control over adjacent territories on the world map.

Chapter 4:. Walkthrough: Main Campaign

Chapter 1: The Yellow Turban Rebellion

The journey begins with the infamous Yellow Turban Rebellion, a massive uprising that threatens the stability of the crumbling Han Dynasty. This chapter introduces players to the basics of the game while immersing them in the chaos of battle. You'll face off against the rebellious Zhang Jiao and his brothers, gaining your first taste of the epic conflicts that define Dynasty Warriors: Origins.

1. Background and Context
The Yellow Turban Rebellion arose from widespread poverty, famine, and discontent among the common people. Led by Zhang Jiao and his brothers, Zhang Bao and Zhang Liang, the rebellion sought to overthrow the corrupt Han court. In this chapter, you'll experience the rebellion's early stages and participate in pivotal battles to suppress it.

2. Objectives and Gameplay
The chapter consists of several missions that guide you through key locations tied to the rebellion. These missions also serve as a tutorial for new players, introducing fundamental mechanics such as

commanding troops, executing combos, and completing objectives.

Mission 1: Suppressing the Uprising
Objective: Eliminate rebel forces attacking key villages.
Gameplay Tips: Use light attacks for swift crowd control and experiment with combos to defeat larger groups. Be sure to protect allied units, as their survival boosts morale.

Mission 2: Capturing Zhang Bao
Objective: Fight through rebel camps to reach Zhang Bao. Defeat him to destabilize the rebels' morale.
Gameplay Tips: Watch for environmental traps in the camps, such as flaming barricades. Use your companions' abilities to clear enemies efficiently.

Mission 3: The Final Battle Against Zhang Jiao
Objective: Confront Zhang Jiao in a climactic showdown at the Yellow Turban stronghold.
Gameplay Tips: Zhang Jiao wields powerful elemental arts, so dodge his attacks and strike during cooldowns. Target his minions to reduce incoming damage and prevent reinforcements.

3. Key Characters and Story Development

This chapter introduces several key figures:

Zhang Jiao: The charismatic leader of the rebellion, Zhang Jiao is a formidable opponent with powerful abilities. Defeating him is your primary goal.

Cao Cao, Sun Jian, and Liu Bei: Emerging as defenders of the Han Dynasty, these leaders begin to showcase their distinct philosophies and strategies. This chapter lays the groundwork for their future conflicts and alliances.

4. Rewards and Progression

Completing this chapter rewards players with:
Increased Morale and Reputation: Boost your standing with factions who view you as a hero of the Han. New Companions: Certain missions unlock companions who join your cause.
Weapons and Resources: Claim loot from fallen enemies and strongholds to upgrade your arsenal.

5. Tips for Success
Focus on Objectives: Prioritize completing main objectives to advance the story, but don't overlook secondary tasks that provide valuable rewards.
Manage Morale: Keeping allied troops alive is crucial for maintaining high morale, which makes battles more manageable. Experiment with Strategies: Use this chapter to familiarize yourself with tactics, such as

ambushing enemies or utilizing environmental elements like fire traps.

The Yellow Turban Rebellion sets the stage for the epic saga of the Three Kingdoms, introducing players to the political and military turmoil of the era. As the rebellion ends, a new threat emerges, paving the way for the rise of ambitious warlords.

Chapter 2: The Rise of Warlords

With the Yellow Turban Rebellion suppressed, the Han Dynasty's fragile peace begins to crumble as ambitious warlords rise to fill the power vacuum. This chapter introduces players to the political intrigue and power struggles that define the Three Kingdoms period. You'll navigate alliances, betrayals, and key battles that set the stage for the larger conflict to come.

1. Background and Context
Following the rebellion, the Han court is weakened and divided, unable to maintain control over its vast territories. Warlords such as Dong Zhuo, Yuan Shao, and Cao Cao emerge as central figures, each vying for dominance. In this chapter, players will witness the fragmentation of power and take part in critical battles that shape the course of history.

2. Objectives and Gameplay

This chapter features multiple missions that highlight the rise of key factions and the increasing complexity of the conflict:

Mission 1: The Siege of Luo Yang

Objective: Defend the Han capital against Dong Zhuo's forces or assist in evacuating key officials.

Gameplay Tips: Use ranged units to fend off attackers and set traps along the city's main gates. Dong Zhuo's forces rely heavily on brute strength, so focus on disrupting their morale.

Mission 2: Yuan Shao's Coalition

Objective: Join Yuan Shao's coalition to confront Dong Zhuo and reclaim Luo Yang.

Gameplay Tips: Coordinate with allied warlords to divide enemy forces. Protect allied leaders like Liu Bei and Sun Jian, as their survival impacts the battle's outcome.

Mission 3: The Betrayal of Lü Bu Objective: Participate in the internal conflict between Dong Zhuo and Lü Bu. Decide whether to align with Lü Bu or remain loyal to the Han court.

Gameplay Tips: If you choose to face Lü Bu, prepare for one of the game's toughest challenges. His combat abilities are unparalleled, requiring precise timing and strategic use of abilities to defeat him.

3. Key Characters and Story Development
This chapter introduces several major figures whose actions will influence the rest of the campaign:

Dong Zhuo: The tyrannical warlord who seizes control of the Han court. His ruthless tactics make him a formidable adversary.
Lü Bu: A fearsome warrior known for his unmatched combat skills and volatile loyalties.
Yuan Shao: The leader of the coalition, whose arrogance and indecision foreshadow future conflicts.
Cao Cao: A rising power whose cunning and ambition begin to take shape as he maneuvers for greater influence.

4. Rewards and Progression
Completing this chapter rewards players with:
New Story Branches: Choices made during this chapter unlock alternate missions and storylines, adding replayability.
Rare Equipment: Defeating high-level enemies like Lü Bu or capturing Dong Zhuo's strongholds provides powerful weapons and armor.
Tactical Insights: Players gain access to advanced strategies, such as deploying decoys and ambushes.

5. Tips for Success

Plan Your Approach: The Rise of Warlords introduces missions with multiple objectives. Prioritize tasks based on your faction's strengths and weaknesses.

Use Allies Wisely: Rely on your companions to hold defensive positions or launch coordinated attacks. Their abilities can complement your playstyle.

Prepare for Lü Bu: If you choose to fight Lü Bu, ensure you've upgraded your weapons and equipped health-restoring items. Focus on evasion and counterattacks to exploit openings in his aggressive style.

Chapter 3: The Battle of Hulao Gate

The Battle of Hulao Gate stands as one of the most iconic moments in the Three Kingdoms saga, pitting the combined forces of the warlords against the tyrannical Dong Zhuo and his formidable champion, Lü Bu. This chapter tests players' skills and strategies, offering one of the first large-scale confrontations of the campaign. The stakes are high, as the outcome of this battle determines the balance of power in the region.

1. Background and Context

Hulao Gate serves as Dong Zhuo's primary stronghold, strategically positioned to block the coalition forces from reaching Luo Yang. Determined to secure his grip on power, Dong Zhuo commands a massive army, with Lü Bu leading the charge as his most fearsome general. The warlords, led by Yuan Shao, must coordinate their efforts to breach the gate and eliminate Dong Zhuo's influence.

2. Objectives and Gameplay
The battle is divided into multiple phases, each with distinct objectives and challenges:

Phase 1: Reaching Hulao Gate
Objective: Clear a path through enemy forces to the gate while securing nearby outposts.
Gameplay Tips: Focus on capturing outposts to weaken enemy reinforcements. Use mounted combat to quickly traverse the battlefield and support allies under heavy attack.

Phase 2: Breaking the Gate
Objective: Deploy siege weapons to destroy Hulao Gate's defenses.
Gameplay Tips: Protect the siege equipment from enemy sabotage. Assign companions to defend key positions while you focus on eliminating enemy officers.

Phase 3: Confronting Lü Bu
Objective: Defeat Lü Bu to break enemy morale and clear the path to Dong Zhuo.

Gameplay Tips: Lü Bu is an exceptionally tough opponent. Use hit-and-run tactics, avoid direct confrontations, and rely on companions to distract him. Timing your Ultimate Arts for maximum damage is crucial.

Phase 4: Pursuing Dong Zhuo
Objective: Dong Zhuo retreats from the battlefield; chase him down to complete the mission.
Gameplay Tips: Focus on speed and avoid unnecessary skirmishes. Use your mount to catch up to Dong Zhuo quickly.

3. Key Characters and Story Development
This chapter further develops the relationships and motivations of key figures:

Lü Bu: Known as the mightiest warrior of his time, Lü Bu's dominance on the battlefield cements his reputation. Players gain insight into his loyalty struggles and relationship with Dong Zhuo.
Dong Zhuo: The tyrant's paranoia and cruelty are on full display as he orders scorched-earth tactics during his retreat.
Warlords of the Coalition: The fragile unity among the warlords begins to show cracks, with disagreements over strategy and recognition foreshadowing future conflicts.

4. Rewards and Progression

Victory in the Battle of Hulao Gate yields significant rewards:

Experience and Resources: Earn experience points for upgrading skills and morale boosts for your faction.

Rare Loot: Defeating Lü Bu may unlock unique weapons or equipment, depending on your difficulty level and performance.

Story Advancements: The aftermath of the battle introduces new alliances, rivalries, and mission paths.

5. Tips for Success

Don't Rush Lü Bu: Avoid engaging Lü Bu too early. Focus on completing other objectives first to weaken his support network.

-Coordinate with Allies: Use the command wheel to assign roles to your companions, ensuring you have support at critical points.

Upgrade Before the Battle: Equip your best gear and abilities before starting this mission, as it is one of the most challenging in the early campaign.

The Battle of Hulao Gate is a defining moment in Dynasty Warriors: Origins, showcasing the scale and intensity of the conflict. With victory, the coalition forces deal a major blow to Dong Zhuo's reign, but the fragile alliances among the warlords begin to unravel, setting the stage for future battles.

Chapter 4: The Formation of Alliances

As the dust settles from the Battle of Hulao Gate, the political landscape of the Three Kingdoms begins to shift dramatically. With Dong Zhuo's forces weakened, the warlords turn their attention toward solidifying their positions and forging alliances to strengthen their claims. This chapter introduces the intricacies of diplomacy, loyalty, and betrayal, with missions that challenge players to balance military prowess and political acumen.

1. Background and Context

The collapse of Dong Zhuo's grip on the Han court creates a power vacuum that the remaining warlords quickly seek to exploit. While some, like Liu Bei, advocate for unity and the restoration of the Han Dynasty, others, such as Cao Cao and Yuan Shao, pursue their ambitions with ruthless pragmatism. In this chapter, players navigate a web of alliances and rivalries that set the stage for the Three Kingdoms' eventual formation.

2. Objectives and Gameplay

This chapter focuses on diplomacy-driven missions, mixed with combat scenarios that test your ability to adapt to changing loyalties and priorities.

Mission 1: Negotiating with Sun Jian
Objective: Convince Sun Jian to align with your faction by assisting him in securing key territories.
Gameplay Tips: This mission emphasizes protecting Sun Jian's forces while completing objectives. Avoid overextending your troops, as enemy reinforcements can appear unexpectedly.

Mission 2: Securing Cao Cao's Support
Objective: Help Cao Cao defend his territories from bandit incursions to earn his favor.
Gameplay Tips: Use a combination of defensive tactics and targeted strikes to protect Cao Cao's supply lines. Coordinating with his forces ensures maximum efficiency.

Mission 3: Betrayal in the Ranks
Objective: Intercept a rebel faction attempting to break an alliance.
Gameplay Tips: Time is critical in this mission. Use mounts to quickly traverse the battlefield and intercept the rebels before they can destabilize your coalition.

3. Key Characters and Story Development

This chapter explores the evolving relationships among the warlords and introduces key moments of character development:

Liu Bei: His idealistic vision of a unified China contrasts sharply with the ambitions of other leaders. His interactions highlight the moral dilemmas of the era.
Cao Cao: As his power grows, so does his reputation for cunning and ruthlessness. Players witness the early stages of his transformation into a dominant force.
Sun Jian: A pragmatic leader, Sun Jian's cooperation depends on mutual benefit. His decisions hint at the eventual rise of the Sun family in the south.

4. Rewards and Progression
Completing this chapter unlocks:

Access to New Allies: Successful negotiations bring new officers and companions into your fold, each with unique skills and abilities.
Strategic Advantages: Gaining control of key territories enhances resource production and troop reinforcements in future battles.
Branching Story Paths: Choices made during this chapter determine which factions remain loyal and influence the trajectory of the campaign.

5. Tips for Success

Balance Combat and Diplomacy: While combat missions are critical, ensuring the success of diplomatic efforts can have long-term benefits.

Use Morale Strategically: High morale among your troops strengthens your negotiating position, making allies more likely to join your cause.

Anticipate Betrayals: Not all alliances are stable. Be prepared to respond quickly if an ally turns against you or if new threats emerge.

Chapter 5: The Battle of Chibi

The Battle of Chibi, also known as the Battle of Red Cliffs, is one of the most defining moments in the Dynasty Warriors: Origins* campaign. This massive naval battle sees the allied forces of Liu Bei and Sun Quan face off against the overwhelming might of Cao Cao's army. Combining strategy, deception, and sheer will, the Battle of Chibi exemplifies the dramatic clashes that shape the Three Kingdoms era.

1. Background and Context

Following the Formation of Alliances, tensions between the factions escalate. Cao Cao, now the most powerful warlord, launches a massive campaign to unify the land under his control. Commanding a fleet of ships and an immense army, he targets the southern territories of Sun

Quan and Liu Bei. Facing annihilation, the two leaders form an alliance and prepare to make their stand at Chibi—a critical chokepoint on the Yangtze River.

The battle's outcome hinges on a daring plan: exploiting Cao Cao's unfamiliarity with naval warfare and turning his strengths against him. Players take center stage in executing this high-risk strategy, shifting the course of history.

2. Objectives and Gameplay
The Battle of Chibi is divided into several stages, each requiring precise execution and coordination.
Phase 1: Establishing Naval Control
Objective: Defend allied ships while weakening Cao Cao's fleet.
Gameplay Tips: Use ranged weapons like bows to target enemy vessels from a safe distance. Protect fire ships as they prepare for deployment.
Phase 2: Preparing the Fire Attack
Objective: Secure the allied base and gather resources for the fire attack.
Gameplay Tips: Capture supply points and defend engineers tasked with constructing fire ships. Keep an eye on reinforcements, as enemy waves increase in intensity.

Phase 3: The Fire Attack

Objective: Launch fire ships into Cao Cao's fleet to inflict massive damage.
Gameplay Tips: Ensure the fire ships reach their targets by eliminating enemy blockades and providing cover for allied units. Timing is critical—coordinate the attack with favorable wind conditions.

Phase 4: Cao Cao's Retreat
Objective: Pursue Cao Cao's fleeing forces to ensure a decisive victory.
Gameplay Tips: Use mounts and fast characters to chase retreating enemies, capturing key officers before they escape. Avoid overextending, as pockets of resistance remain.

3. Key Characters and Story Development
The Battle of Chibi highlights the contrasting leadership styles and motivations of the factions:

Liu Bei: His commitment to justice and the people drives him to stand against overwhelming odds.
Sun Quan: A pragmatic leader, Sun Quan's decision to ally with Liu Bei reflects his understanding of mutual survival.
Cao Cao: Arrogant yet brilliant, Cao Cao's overconfidence and inexperience with naval warfare lead to his downfall.

The battle also introduces notable figures like Zhou Yu, whose strategic genius is instrumental in planning the fire attack.

4. Rewards and Progression
Victory at Chibi provides substantial rewards:
New Abilities and Weapons: Completing objectives unlocks rare gear and advanced skills for key characters.
Territorial Gains: The successful defense of the south shifts the balance of power, opening new regions to explore.
Story Advancement: The alliances forged during Chibi solidify the foundations of Wu and Shu, setting the stage for future conflicts.

5. Tips for Success

Master Naval Combat: Adjust your tactics for ship-based battles, focusing on mobility and range.
Protect Key Units: Losing fire ships or engineers can lead to mission failure. Prioritize their safety during critical stages.
Coordinate with Allies: Assign companions to defend vital positions while you execute offensive maneuvers.

Decision Points and Multiple Endings

One of the standout features of Dynasty Warriors: Origins is the inclusion of decision points that influence the storyline and unlock multiple endings. These choices add depth and replayability to the game, allowing players to shape the fate of the Three Kingdoms based on their actions and alliances. This subchapter explores the decision-making mechanics, their impact on the narrative, and how to unlock the various endings.

1. The Role of Decision Points

Throughout the campaign, players encounter key moments where their choices affect the story. These decision points are not always obvious, often embedded in dialogue, battle outcomes, or side quests. The consequences of these choices can be immediate or ripple across later chapters.

Types of Decisions:
Dialogue Choices: Responses in conversations with key characters influence alliances and personal relationships.
Battlefield Decisions: Choosing which objectives to prioritize or how to approach a battle can determine the survival of allies or the outcome of the war.
Faction Alignments: Deciding which faction to support during pivotal moments significantly alters the storyline.

2. Impact on the Storyline

The decisions you make shape the course of the Three Kingdoms, from the formation of alliances to the rise and fall of key leaders.

Alliances: Supporting Liu Bei, Cao Cao, or Sun Quan leads to diverging storylines, missions, and character interactions.
Character Outcomes: Certain choices determine whether companions remain loyal, defect, or even survive.
Territorial Control: The regions you prioritize influence the map and resource availability in later chapters.

3. The Multiple Endings
Dynasty Warriors: Origins features several endings, each reflecting the player's decisions throughout the campaign.
The Unification Ending: Achieved by aligning with one faction (Wei, Wu, or Shu) and leading it to dominance over the other two. This ending highlights the chosen faction's vision for a unified China. The Balanced Ending: Secured by fostering cooperation among the factions and maintaining a fragile peace. This ending emphasizes diplomacy and mutual survival.
The Chaos Ending: Triggered by betraying allies and prioritizing personal power over unity. This ending portrays a fractured China where no one emerges as the ultimate victor.

4. Unlocking Endings and Hidden Content

To unlock all endings and hidden content, players must carefully manage their choices and actions:

Replay Missions: Use the Free Mode feature to revisit earlier chapters and make different decisions.

Complete Side Quests: Many decision points are tied to optional missions that influence character relationships and resources.

Track Relationship Levels: High affinity with certain characters unlocks exclusive dialogue and alternate missions.

5. Tips for Navigating Decision Points

Pay Attention to Dialogue: NPCs often provide subtle hints about the consequences of your choices.

Balance Short-Term and Long-Term Goals: While immediate rewards may seem appealing, some decisions have far-reaching consequences that can affect later chapters.

Experiment with Playthroughs: To experience all the endings, focus on a single faction or philosophy in each playthrough.

6. The Significance of Player Choice

The decision-making system in Dynasty Warriors: Origins elevates the campaign, making players feel like active participants in the story. By choosing who to ally with, what battles to fight, and which objectives to prioritize, players craft their unique version of the Three Kingdoms saga.

Chapter 5 Characters and Companions

Overview of Playable Characters

The diverse cast of playable characters in Dynasty Warriors: Origins brings the epic Three Kingdoms saga to life. Each character is intricately designed, with unique abilities, weapons, and storylines that cater to different playstyles. From legendary warlords to rising heroes, this chapter explores the personalities, strengths, and contributions of the game's key characters.

1. The Main Heroes

Liu Bei:
Faction: Shu
Weapon: Dual Swords
Playstyle: Balanced and versatile, Liu Bei excels at both offense and defense, making him ideal for players new to the series.
Personality: A compassionate and idealistic leader, Liu Bei strives to restore justice and harmony to the land.

Cao Cao:
Faction: Wei
Weapon: Straight Sword

Playstyle: Strategic and calculated, Cao Cao's abilities focus on controlling the battlefield and enhancing troop morale.
Personality: Charismatic and pragmatic, Cao Cao's ambition drives him to unite China under his rule, regardless of the cost.

Sun Jian:
Faction: Wu
Weapon: Long Sword
Playstyle: Aggressive and fast-paced, Sun Jian thrives in high-pressure combat situations.
Personality: A fearless warrior and loyal leader, Sun Jian's vision for a strong and independent Wu shapes his actions.

2. Notable Supporting Characters
Zhao Yun:
Faction: Shu
Weapon: Spear
Playstyle: Agile and precise, Zhao Yun specializes in crowd control and quick strikes.
Personality: A loyal and honorable warrior, Zhao Yun embodies the ideals of Shu and is fiercely devoted to Liu Bei.

Diao Chan:
Faction: Independent

Weapon: Whip

Playstyle: Graceful and deceptive, Diao Chan uses elegant combos to confuse enemies and deal critical damage.

Personality: Driven by a desire to end tyranny, Diao Chan's cunning plays a pivotal role in key political intrigues.

Lü Bu:

Faction: Independent

Weapon: Halberd

Playstyle: A powerhouse character, Lü Bu excels in dealing massive damage but requires careful stamina management.

Personality: Fearless and unpredictable, Lü Bu's ambition and unmatched skill make him a force to be reckoned with.

3. Custom Characters

For players seeking a personalized experience, Dynasty Warriors: Origins offers a custom character creation system. Players can design their hero's appearance, choose a weapon type, and assign abilities. These custom characters seamlessly integrate into the campaign, offering a fresh perspective on the classic story.

4. Choosing the Right Character for Your Playstyle

Each playable character is tailored to specific combat preferences:
For Beginners: Characters like Liu Bei and Zhao Yun provide balanced skill sets and straightforward mechanics.
For Aggressive Players: Sun Jian and Lü Bu cater to those who prefer high-risk, high-reward combat styles.
For Strategic Players: Cao Cao and Diao Chan offer abilities that emphasize battlefield control and finesse.

5. Unlocking Additional Playable Characters
As the campaign progresses, players unlock new characters through story events, completing side missions, and achieving specific milestones. Each new character adds depth to the roster, ensuring a dynamic and evolving gameplay experience.

Companion Abilities and Roles

Companions in Dynasty Warriors: Origins play a vital role in both combat and story progression. Each companion brings unique abilities, strengths, and tactical advantages, allowing players to customize their approach to battles and missions. Understanding their roles and how to utilize their abilities effectively is key to success.

1. Types of Companions and Their Roles

Companions are categorized into distinct roles based on their combat style and utility on the battlefield.

Offensive Companions:
Examples: Lü Bu, Guan Yu, Sun Ce
Role: These companions excel in dealing high damage, targeting key enemy officers, and breaking through defenses.
Abilities:
Lü Bu's "Fury Strike" unleashes a devastating area-of-effect attack.
Guan Yu's "Momentum Charge" increases his attack speed and power temporarily.

Defensive Companions:
Examples: Zhang Fei, Xu Huang, Xiahou Dun
Role: Defensive companions protect allied units, hold critical positions, and absorb damage.
Abilities:
Zhang Fei's "Unyielding Wall" creates a shield that reduces incoming damage for nearby allies.
Xu Huang's "Fortified Stance" boosts his defense while drawing enemy aggression.

Supportive Companions:
Examples: Zhuge Liang, Diao Chan, Huang Zhong
Role: Support companions provide buffs, healing, or ranged assistance to the player and allies.

Abilities:
Zhuge Liang's "Strategic Command" enhances morale and troop effectiveness.
Diao Chan's "Inspiring Dance" heals allies and boosts their attack temporarily.

Hybrid Companions:
Examples: Zhao Yun, Sun Shangxiang, Sima Yi
Role: Hybrid companions offer a mix of offensive and defensive capabilities, making them versatile for various situations.
Abilities:
Zhao Yun's "Dragon Charge" combines mobility and power for swift enemy elimination. Sun Shangxiang's "Arrow Storm" delivers sustained ranged attacks while evading enemy strikes.

2. Companion Abilities in Combat

Companions bring unique skills that complement the player's strategy:
Active Abilities:
Triggered abilities that deal significant damage, provide crowd control, or enhance the player's effectiveness. Timing these abilities during critical moments can turn the tide of battle.

Passive Traits:

Companions have inherent bonuses that activate when they're in your party. For example, Guan Yu increases the player's attack power, while Zhuge Liang improves resource gathering rates.

Combo Attacks: By building affinity with companions, players can unlock devastating combo attacks. These synchronized moves combine the strengths of the player and companion, dealing massive damage.

3. Tactical Deployment of Companions

The effectiveness of companions depends on how they're deployed on the battlefield:

Assigned Roles: Use the command wheel to direct companions to specific tasks, such as holding a defensive position or leading an assault on enemy strongholds. Synergy with Player Skills: Pairing companions whose abilities complement your character's playstyle enhances overall effectiveness. For example, a defensive player might benefit from offensive companions like Lü Bu or Guan Yu.

4. Managing Companion Affinity

Affinity levels measure the strength of your bond with companions. High affinity unlocks new abilities, dialogue, and exclusive story content.

- Increasing Affinity:
- Complete missions with companions.
- Engage in dialogue and fulfill their requests.
- Defend them during battles or prioritize their objectives.

Affinity Rewards:
Unlock new combo attacks and support abilities.
Gain access to personal story missions that deepen the companion's backstory.

5. Tips for Companion Management
Balance Your Team: Ensure a mix of offensive, defensive, and support companions to handle a variety of scenarios.
Rotate Companions: Regularly switch companions to unlock their abilities and improve affinity across your roster.
Leverage Morale: Assign companions to high-morale units to maximize their impact on the battlefield.

Building Bonds and Relationships
In Dynasty Warriors: Origins relationships with your companions are more than just a narrative element—they directly influence gameplay, providing unique abilities, enhanced teamwork, and exclusive story arcs. Building strong bonds with your allies adds depth to the

experience and offers tangible benefits on the battlefield. This subchapter explores how to strengthen relationships, the rewards of high affinity, and the impact these bonds have on the overarching story.

1. Understanding Affinity Levels

Affinity represents the bond between you and your companions, measured on a scale ranging from neutral to deep trust. Higher affinity levels unlock new abilities, dialogue options, and special missions that deepen the lore of the Three Kingdoms.

Affinity Tiers: Neutral: Default state when a companion joins your party.
Friendly: Minor improvements in teamwork and battlefield coordination.
Trusted: Unlocks advanced combo attacks and story interactions.
Bonded: Maximum affinity level, granting exclusive abilities and narrative outcomes.

2. Ways to Build Bonds
Strengthening relationships requires consistent interaction and thoughtful actions. Here are the primary methods:

Combat Performance:

Complete missions with companions to increase affinity. Protect them during battles by intercepting threats and healing them when necessary.

Dialogue and Interactions:
Speak with companions in camp or during downtime between missions.
Choose dialogue options that align with their values and personality.
Engage in personal quests to show commitment to their cause.

Gifts and Tokens:
Certain items found during exploration or earned as rewards can be gifted to companions.
Each companion has specific preferences—for example, Zhuge Liang appreciates strategy-related artifacts, while Zhao Yun values heroic memorabilia.

Mission Decisions:
Supporting a companion's viewpoint during critical decisions boosts their affinity.
Siding against their beliefs can decrease it, potentially straining your relationship.

3. Benefits of Strong Bonds

High affinity with companions provides numerous advantages, both in gameplay and storytelling:

Enhanced Abilities:
Unlock unique passive traits and active skills exclusive to bonded companions.
Increase the effectiveness of combo attacks and coordinated maneuvers.

Personal Missions: High affinity grants access to character-specific missions that delve into their backstories. Completing these missions often rewards rare equipment or additional storyline insights.

Improved Morale and Teamwork: Companions with strong bonds are more effective in battle, boosting allied morale and providing greater support.

Narrative Impact:
Relationships can influence major story events and endings. For instance, trusted companions may choose to stay loyal even in difficult circumstances, while neglected ones might leave or betray your cause.

4. Managing Relationship Challenges
While building bonds is rewarding, maintaining them requires care: Conflict Resolution: Disagreements

between companions can arise during missions. Mediating these conflicts strengthens relationships across the group.
Ignoring conflicts or choosing divisive options can lead to strained bonds.

Balancing Focus: Rotate companions regularly to ensure balanced affinity growth. Neglecting certain characters may limit their availability or effectiveness later in the game.

Repairing Damaged Bonds:
If affinity decreases, perform actions that align with the companion's values or prioritize their objectives in missions.

5. Building Bonds Beyond the Battlefield

The camp system allows for deeper interactions, creating opportunities to bond in non-combat settings:

Training Sessions: Participate in training exercises with companions to improve their skills and strengthen your bond.
Campfire Dialogues: Use downtime to engage in personal conversations, uncovering hidden aspects of their personalities.

6. Tips for Maximizing Relationships

Learn Companion Preferences: Understanding each character's personality and values ensures you make choices that resonate with them.

Prioritize Personal Quests: Completing these missions not only enhances affinity but also rewards valuable items and insights.

Monitor Affinity Progress: Use the companion menu to track relationship levels and plan actions to strengthen weaker bonds.

Unlocking Additional Characters

One of the most exciting aspects of Dynasty Warriors: Origins is the ability to expand your roster of characters. Unlocking additional characters not only diversifies gameplay but also opens new storylines, abilities, and strategies. This subchapter outlines how to recruit new allies, the requirements for unlocking hidden characters, and the benefits of a growing roster.

1. Main Story Unlocks

The majority of new characters are introduced naturally through the main campaign. Completing specific chapters or missions often results in key historical figures joining your cause.

Example Unlocks by Campaign Progress:

Zhao Yun: Joins early in the Shu storyline during the Yellow Turban Rebellion.
Sun Shangxiang: Becomes available after completing the Battle of Chibi in the Wu campaign.
Xu Huang: Unlocks mid-campaign in the Wei storyline after defeating rival factions.
Tips: Focus on progressing through the main story to gain access to key faction leaders and warriors.

2. Side Missions and Quests

Many characters are unlocked through optional side missions that require specific actions or objectives to be completed.

Special Unlock Quests:
Pang Tong: Requires players to defend an allied base during an ambush mission.
Diao Chan: Unlocked by completing her personal quest, which involves destabilizing Dong Zhuo's regime.
Tips: Keep an eye out for optional missions on the world map, as they often lead to character unlock opportunities.

3. Decision-Based Unlocks

Certain characters only become available based on the decisions you make during the campaign. Aligning with specific factions or choosing particular dialogue options can influence who joins your cause.

Examples of Decision-Based Characters:
Lü Bu: Can be recruited if you choose to support him during his conflict with Dong Zhuo.
Zhang Fei: His allegiance depends on your support of Liu Bei's ideals in critical moments.

Tips: Replay missions and experiment with different choices to unlock all potential recruits.

4. Hidden and Secret Characters
For players seeking a challenge, Dynasty Warriors: Origins includes several hidden characters that require meeting specific conditions to unlock.

Unlock Criteria for Hidden Characters:
Zhuge Liang: Complete all missions in the Shu campaign with an S rank.
Gan Ning: Capture a series of naval bases during the Wu storyline.
Dong Zhuo: Defeat him in a high-difficulty setting and choose to spare him during a story event.
Tips: Hidden characters often require exceptional performance or exploration of alternate story paths. Focus on achieving high rankings and completing optional objectives.

5. Custom Characters

In addition to historical figures, players can create their own custom characters. Unlocking additional customization options, such as new weapons, armor styles, and abilities, often ties to campaign progress and achievements.

Customization Unlocks:
New outfits and accessories are awarded for completing faction-specific storylines.
Additional skill trees and weapon styles become available as you level up existing characters.

6. Multiplayer Unlocks

Certain characters and skins are exclusive to multiplayer or co-op modes. Participating in online battles and completing cooperative objectives can unlock unique rewards.

Examples:
Special variants of Cao Cao and Liu Bei with unique abilities.
Exclusive weapons and cosmetics for online participation.
Tips: Engage in multiplayer to diversify your roster and gain rare items.

7. Benefits of Unlocking Additional Characters

Expanding your roster provides:
Diverse Playstyles: Each character offers a unique combat experience, from agile fighters to heavy-hitting tanks.
Strategic Flexibility: A larger roster allows for tailored teams to tackle specific missions or challenges.
Enhanced Replayability: With more characters, players can explore different perspectives and alternate storylines.

Chapter 6: Weapons and Equipment

Weapon Acquisition and Upgrades

Weapons play a pivotal role in defining your combat style and effectiveness in Dynasty Warriors: Origins. Acquiring and upgrading weapons not only enhances your character's power but also provides new strategies and combos for tackling challenging battles. This subchapter explores the methods for obtaining weapons, the upgrade system, and how to maximize their potential.

1. Methods of Weapon Acquisition
Weapons can be obtained through various means, ensuring a steady progression throughout the campaign:
Defeating Enemies:
Defeated officers and commanders often drop weapons as rewards. Higher-ranked enemies provide better-quality weapons, especially when defeated in high-difficulty settings.

Mission Rewards:
Completing main story missions, side quests, and optional challenges often rewards players with new weapons. Bonus objectives within missions can yield rare or unique equipment.

Treasure Chests: Certain battlefields feature hidden treasure chests containing weapons. Use the battlefield map to locate these and prioritize capturing areas where treasures are likely to spawn.

Blacksmiths and Merchants: Visit blacksmiths in towns or camps to purchase weapons. Merchants sometimes sell rare or special weapons for in-game currency or unique materials.

2. Weapon Rarity and Quality

Weapons are classified by rarity, which affects their base stats and potential for upgrades:

Common Weapons: Standard equipment with modest stats, suitable for early-game progression.
Uncommon Weapons: Offer improved stats and may include a single trait.
Rare Weapons: High-damage weapons with multiple traits, often obtained through challenging missions.
Legendary Weapons: The most powerful weapons, featuring unique appearances and abilities. These are typically unlocked by completing story arcs, achieving S-rank missions, or defeating special enemies.

3. The Upgrade System

Upgrading weapons allows players to enhance their stats and unlock additional features. Upgrades require specific materials, which can be found through exploration, combat, or trading with merchants.

Upgrade Tiers:
Each weapon has several upgrade levels, increasing its attack power, durability, and trait effectiveness.
Higher-tier upgrades require rarer materials, such as ores or special drops from elite enemies.

Enhancing Traits: Upgrades can also improve weapon traits, such as boosting elemental damage or increasing critical hit rates.

Refinement Options:
Players can refine weapons to change their attributes or add new traits. Refinement is especially useful for tailoring weapons to specific battles or playstyles.

4. Crafting Custom Weapons
In addition to acquiring and upgrading existing weapons, players can craft custom weapons by gathering blueprints and materials:

Blueprints:
Found in treasure chests, earned as mission rewards, or purchased from merchants.

Materials:

Gather materials such as iron, jade, or rare crystals from resource nodes and defeated enemies.

Crafting allows players to design weapons with specific traits and elemental properties, ensuring a personalized combat experience.

5. Tips for Efficient Weapon Management

Keep a Balanced Arsenal: Carry weapons suited for different combat scenarios, such as crowd control or single-target damage.

Sell or Recycle Unused Weapons: Clear inventory space and earn additional resources by trading in lower-quality equipment.

Focus on Synergy: Pair weapons with your character's abilities or companion skills to maximize efficiency in battle.

Traits and Customization Options

The weapon system in Dynasty Warriors: Origins offers a wealth of customization options, allowing players to tailor their equipment to their playstyle and strategic needs. Weapon traits enhance combat effectiveness by adding unique effects and bonuses, while customization options provide the freedom to create personalized and powerful arsenals. This subchapter explores the traits system, customization mechanics, and how to optimize weapons for maximum efficiency.

1. Weapon Traits Overview
Weapon traits are special attributes that provide passive or active bonuses during combat. Traits are tied to specific weapons and can be enhanced or swapped through refinement.

Common Traits:
Critical Boost: Increases critical hit chance or damage.
Life Steal: Restores health with each successful hit.
Stamina Recovery: Speeds up stamina regeneration during battle.

Elemental Traits:
Fire: Adds burn damage over time, effective against armored foes.
Ice: Slows enemies on hit, providing crowd control.
Lightning: Stuns enemies temporarily, disrupting their attacks.
Unique Traits: Revenge Strike: Increases damage output after taking a hit.
Chain Effect: Boosts combo multiplier for each successive attack.
Shield Breaker: Enhances damage against shielded or heavily armored opponents.

Tips: Choose traits that align with your character's strengths and the challenges of upcoming battles.

2. Customization Options
Customization in *Dynasty Warriors: Origins* allows players to modify their weapons to suit different scenarios:

Refinement:
Replace or enhance existing traits by using materials and currency. Refinement is particularly useful for creating specialized weapons, such as those focused on elemental damage or critical hits.

Socketing Gems:
Some weapons feature gem slots that provide additional bonuses. Gems can be found during exploration or crafted using rare materials.
Examples of Gem Effects:
Attack Gem: Increases base damage.
Defense Gem: Reduces incoming damage.
Elemental Gem: Amplifies elemental effects like fire or ice.

Reforging:
Allows players to re-roll weapon stats or traits for a chance to improve overall quality.

Requires a mix of standard and rare materials, encouraging exploration and resource management.

3. Customization Based on Playstyle

Customization is most effective when tailored to your preferred combat approach:

Offensive Builds:
Focus on traits like Critical Boost, Attack Gem socketing, and elemental damage. Example Weapon: A fire-enhanced greatsword with high attack power and critical bonuses.

Defensive Builds:
Emphasize traits like Stamina Recovery, Defense Gems, and Life Steal.
Example Weapon: A shield-enhanced axe designed for absorbing and retaliating damage.

Balanced Builds:
Combine traits and gems for versatility across various combat scenarios. Example Weapon: A spear with lightning damage, moderate critical bonuses, and stamina regeneration.

4. Obtaining Customization Materials

Customization materials are essential for upgrading and refining weapons. They can be obtained through:

Battlefield Resources: Found in treasure chests, resource nodes, and as drops from elite enemies.
Quests and Rewards: Side missions and main campaign objectives often yield rare materials.
Trading with Merchants: Purchase hard-to-find materials using in-game currency or trade items.

Tips: Prioritize missions and areas known for rare material drops when planning upgrades.

5. Advanced Customization Strategies

Optimize for Specific Battles: Analyze the enemy types and terrain of upcoming missions to equip weapons with appropriate traits and elemental damage.
Adapt Mid-Campaign: As enemy difficulty increases, refine or reforge your weapons to keep up with the challenge.
Experiment with Combinations: Test different traits and gem setups to discover synergies that enhance your playstyle.

6. Benefits of Weapon Customization

Investing in weapon customization yields significant advantages:

- Increased combat efficiency and damage output.
-Greater adaptability to different mission objectives and enemy types.
-Enhanced replayability by allowing experimentation with various builds and strategies.

Purchasing and Finding Rare Weapons

Rare weapons are among the most powerful tools in Dynasty Warriors: Origins, offering enhanced stats, unique traits, and a distinct visual flair. Obtaining these rare weapons often requires a mix of exploration, combat prowess, and resource management. This subchapter focuses on how to purchase, find, and unlock rare weapons, ensuring you build a formidable arsenal.

1. Purchasing Rare Weapons

Rare weapons can be acquired from merchants and blacksmiths in towns, camps, or during specific missions.

Merchants: Stock Availability: Merchants occasionally stock rare weapons, with inventory cycling based on story progression or player achievements.

Requirements:
Rare weapons are typically more expensive than standard equipment, requiring a substantial amount of in-game currency.
Some merchants trade rare weapons for specific materials or artifacts instead of currency.

Blacksmith Upgrades:
Blacksmiths often sell exclusive weapons if you've invested in upgrading their facilities.
Completing certain missions or side quests for blacksmiths may unlock rare items in their inventory.
Tips: Visit merchants and blacksmiths regularly to check for new stock, and save your resources for high-quality purchases.

2. Finding Rare Weapons on the Battlefield

Exploration and battle performance are key to uncovering rare weapons:
Enemy Officers and Commanders:
Defeating high-ranking enemy officers often rewards players with rare or unique weapons.
Boss fights or legendary enemies are prime sources for obtaining top-tier equipment.
Treasure Chests:
Rare weapons are hidden in treasure chests scattered across the battlefield.

Use the mini-map or scout companions to locate chest markers during missions.

Dynamic Events:
Special events, such as ambushes or reinforcements, may trigger opportunities to claim rare weapons.
Completing timed objectives, such as intercepting an enemy supply caravan, often yields rare loot.

3. Quest Rewards
Many rare weapons are tied to completing specific missions or optional challenges:

Storyline Rewards:
Main campaign missions often grant rare weapons as rewards, particularly after pivotal battles or defeating major characters.
Example: Defeating Lü Bu at Hulao Gate might reward players with a legendary halberd.

Side Quests:
Optional missions frequently provide rare weapons as a reward for outstanding performance or achieving bonus objectives.
Example: Capturing a strategic base within a time limit could unlock a unique spear or bow.

Faction Objectives: Aligning with certain factions and completing their unique objectives can unlock faction-themed rare weapons.

4. Special Events and Challenges

Time-Limited Events: Occasionally, the game introduces time-limited missions or online events that offer exclusive rare weapons. Participating in these events provides access to gear unavailable elsewhere.

Arena Challenges:
Test your skills in the game's arena mode, where high scores and flawless victories can reward rare weapons.

Exploration Zones:
Certain open-world areas or hidden dungeons house powerful enemies and treasure troves. Successfully exploring these zones often leads to rare equipment.

5. Crafting Rare Weapons
If you cannot find or purchase a specific weapon, crafting offers another route:
Blueprints: Obtain blueprints for rare weapons by completing missions, opening treasure chests, or trading with NPCs.

Unique Materials: Rare weapons require hard-to-find crafting materials, often dropped by elite enemies or gathered from rare resource nodes.
Blacksmith Crafting: Visit upgraded blacksmiths to craft rare weapons using the blueprints and materials you've collected.

6. Maximizing Rare Weapon Drops

Players can improve their chances of finding rare weapons by adopting specific strategies:
Difficulty Settings: Playing on higher difficulty levels increases the likelihood of rare weapon drops from enemies.
Luck Stat and Boosts: Certain items or traits enhance your luck, improving the quality of loot obtained during missions.
Replay Missions: Use Free Mode to replay missions with rare weapon rewards, focusing on achieving higher ranks or completing additional objectives.

7. Benefits of Rare Weapons
Rare weapons provide significant advantages:
Enhanced stats that outperform common or uncommon weapons.
Unique traits that can turn the tide of challenging battles.
Visual customization options that add style and flair to your character.

Equipment Strategies for Different Battles

The choice of weapons and equipment in *Dynasty Warriors: Origins can greatly influence the outcome of battles. Each mission presents unique challenges, from vast open plains to tightly packed urban skirmishes, and tailoring your arsenal to the battlefield is crucial. This subchapter explores effective equipment strategies for various battle scenarios, helping players optimize their performance.

1. Understanding Battlefield Types
Each battlefield type requires a distinct approach to equipment selection:

Open Plains:
Challenges: Large groups of enemies, wide spaces with limited cover.
Recommended Equipment:
Polearms or Spears: Their wide attack range is perfect for crowd control.
Mount-Friendly Gear: Equip items that enhance mounted combat, as horses are ideal for traversing open terrain quickly.
Traits: Focus on stamina regeneration and increased attack range to maintain momentum.

Urban Environments:

Challenges: Narrow pathways, chokepoints, and ambushes.
Recommended Equipment:
Short Swords or Dual Blades: Fast weapons that excel in tight quarters.
Defensive Traits: Traits like Shield Breaker and increased parry effectiveness are crucial for handling ambushes.
Elemental Effects: Fire traits can create chaos in confined spaces, forcing enemies into disarray.

Siege Battles:
Challenges: Strongholds with high fortitude, ranged defenses, and prolonged engagements.
Recommended Equipment:
Heavy Weapons: Great Axes or Hammers to break gates and stronghold defenses.
Supportive Traits: Healing effects and stamina recovery help sustain long fights.
Ranged Weapons: Bows or crossbows to eliminate defenders on walls or towers.

Naval Combat:
Challenges: Restricted movement and reliance on ranged tactics.
Recommended Equipment:
Ranged Weapons: Equip bows or dual crossbows to dominate ship-based combat.

Lightning Traits: Stun enemies for easier elimination on narrow decks.

Mobility Enhancements: Traits that reduce stamina cost for dashing or evading are essential.

2. Equipment Loadouts for Enemy Types

Tailor your equipment to the types of enemies you'll face:

Armored Enemies:
Use weapons with Shield Breaker or Armor Piercing traits to bypass defenses.
Elemental traits like Lightning or Fire are effective at disrupting heavily armored foes.

Elite Officers:
Equip weapons with high critical hit rates or Life Steal to sustain longer duels. Traits like Revenge Strike can amplify damage when fighting stronger opponents.

Hordes of Troops:
Opt for polearms, spears, or other weapons with wide-area attacks to clear groups efficiently.
Traits like Chain Effect boost combo potential, keeping hordes at bay.

3. Adapting to Mission Objectives

Assault Missions: Prioritize offensive traits and weapons with high damage output to quickly capture objectives.
Defensive Missions: Equip shields or defensive weapons, and use traits that increase fortitude and stamina recovery to outlast enemy waves.
Escort Missions: Use fast weapons and traits that enhance mobility to stay close to the escorted unit while fending off enemies.

4. Balancing Companions and Equipment
Coordinate your equipment with your companions' abilities to maximize team efficiency:

Offensive Allies: Equip defensive or supportive gear to complement their aggressive playstyle.
Defensive Allies: Use high-damage weapons to compensate for their slower combat pace.
Ranged Allies: Pair with close-range weapons to ensure balanced coverage of the battlefield.

5. Leveraging Traits for Specific Strategies
Aggression: Use traits like Critical Boost and Fire Element for high damage output in fast-paced missions.
Control: Equip Lightning or Ice traits to immobilize enemies and maintain battlefield control.

Sustainability: Life Steal and Stamina Recovery traits ensure you can endure prolonged engagements without faltering.

6. Preparing for Boss Battles

Boss encounters require specialized equipment strategies:
Equip weapons with traits that increase damage against single targets.
Use ranged or elemental weapons to exploit boss weaknesses or disrupt their attack patterns. Prioritize defensive traits if the boss uses overwhelming attacks, ensuring survivability.

7. Tips for Equipment Optimization
Test Loadouts: Experiment with different equipment combinations in Free Mode to find what works best for your playstyle.
Upgrade and Refine: Continuously improve your weapons to keep pace with increasing difficulty levels.
Analyze the Battlefield: Review mission details to anticipate challenges and prepare accordingly.

Chapter 7. Side Missions and Activities

Missions: Objectives and Rewards

Side missions in Dynasty Warriors: Origins offer a wealth of opportunities to explore the world, earn valuable rewards, and uncover hidden aspects of the story. These optional objectives range from assisting allies in battle to completing unique challenges that test your skills and strategy. This subchapter provides a detailed look at the types of side missions, their objectives, and the rewards they offer.

1. Types of Side Missions

Side missions are designed to complement the main campaign while offering unique gameplay experiences:

Combat Missions: Focused on defeating specific enemies or completing objectives within a time limit.
Examples:
Eliminate an elite officer before reinforcements arrive.
Defend an allied base from waves of attackers.

Escort Missions:

Tasked with protecting NPCs or supply caravans as they move through dangerous territories.
Tips: Use fast weapons and mobility traits to stay ahead of ambushes.

Resource Collection Missions:
Gather materials or secure supply points to strengthen your faction.
Examples:
Harvest resources from enemy-controlled mines.
Capture a caravan transporting rare goods.

Investigation Missions:
Involve exploring areas, locating hidden items, or uncovering enemy plans.
Examples:
Scout an enemy camp and report their numbers.
Retrieve a lost artifact from a dangerous region.

2. Objectives in Side Missions

Side missions often include both primary and secondary objectives:
Primary Objectives:
Completing the main goal of the mission is necessary for success.
Examples: Defeating a key enemy officer or defending an allied position.

Secondary Objectives:
Optional tasks that provide bonus rewards if completed.
Examples: Achieving a time-based challenge, rescuing allies, or defeating a certain number of enemies.
Tips: Prioritize secondary objectives when possible to maximize rewards, but ensure they don't interfere with completing the primary mission.

3. Rewards for Side Missions

Side missions offer a variety of rewards that enhance your characters and arsenal:
Experience Points: Help level up your character and companions, unlocking new abilities and skill upgrades.
Weapons and Equipment: Rare and unique items are often tied to side missions, providing significant advantages in later battles.
Materials and Resources: Essential for crafting, refining, and upgrading weapons.
Currency: In-game money earned from side missions can be spent at merchants or blacksmiths.
Story Content: Some side missions reveal additional lore, character backstories, or hidden narrative branches.

4. Replayability of Side Missions

Side missions can be replayed in Free Mode, offering opportunities to:
Achieve higher rankings for better rewards.
Experiment with different characters and strategies.
Discover alternate outcomes or secrets tied to the mission.

5. Tips for Success in Side Missions

Prepare Strategically: Equip weapons and traits suited to the mission type and anticipated challenges.
Bring the Right Companions: Choose allies whose abilities complement your objectives, such as defensive companions for escort missions or offensive ones for combat-heavy tasks. Manage Time Wisely: Some missions include tight time limits, so prioritize efficiency and mobility.
Explore Thoroughly: Keep an eye out for hidden treasure chests or resources that can provide additional rewards.

Skirmishes: Challenges and Strategies

Skirmishes in Dynasty Warriors: Origins are optional, high-intensity encounters that test your combat skills, strategic thinking, and adaptability. These battles often occur outside the main campaign and offer unique challenges, valuable rewards, and opportunities to experiment with different tactics. This subchapter delves into the mechanics of skirmishes, the types of challenges you'll face, and strategies for success.

1. What Are Skirmishes?
Skirmishes are smaller-scale battles that focus on specific objectives or conditions. They serve as an excellent way to gain experience, refine skills, and earn rare items.
Dynamic Challenges: Skirmishes often have unpredictable elements, such as enemy reinforcements, time constraints, or environmental hazards.
Replayable Content: These missions can be revisited to improve your performance or achieve bonus objectives.

2. Types of Skirmishes
Skirmishes come in various formats, each offering distinct gameplay experiences:

Survival Challenges:
Objective: Survive waves of increasingly difficult enemies.
Strategy: Prioritize crowd control weapons and traits like Stamina Recovery to maintain energy throughout prolonged engagements.
Officer Duels:
Objective: Defeat a series of elite enemy officers in one-on-one or small-group battles.

Strategy: Equip weapons with high single-target damage and traits like Critical Boost for maximum effectiveness.

Timed Assaults:
Objective: Eliminate a set number of enemies or complete objectives within a strict time limit.
Strategy: Focus on mobility and area-of-effect attacks to clear enemies quickly.
Defensive Stand:
Objective: Protect an allied position or NPC from enemy forces.
Strategy: Use defensive companions and weapons with crowd control traits to hold the line.

Ambush Missions:
Objective: Intercept enemy forces or disrupt their plans.
Strategy: Utilize mounts or traits that boost movement speed to respond quickly to threats.

3. Rewards for Skirmishes
Skirmishes are a rich source of valuable rewards:
Rare Weapons and Traits: High-ranking skirmishes often reward players with powerful equipment.
Skill Points: Completing skirmishes grants experience that can be used to unlock or upgrade abilities.
Crafting Materials: Rare materials needed for weapon upgrades are frequently found in skirmish missions.

Cosmetic Items: Special skirmishes may reward exclusive character skins or customization options.

4. Strategies for Skirmish Success

Analyze the Objective: Understand the mission goal before starting. Focus your efforts on the primary objective, but aim for bonus goals if they're achievable.
Tailor Your Loadout: Equip weapons and traits suited to the skirmish type. For example, bring ranged weapons for ambushes or high-damage weapons for officer duels.
Use Companions Effectively: Assign roles to your companions based on their abilities. Defensive companions can hold positions, while offensive allies excel in assaults.
Master the Terrain: Skirmishes often include environmental challenges. Use high ground, narrow chokepoints, or destructible objects to gain an advantage.
Manage Resources: Conserve stamina and health items for critical moments, especially in survival or timed skirmishes.

5. Advanced Skirmishes and Elite Challenges
As you progress, advanced skirmishes and elite challenges become available, offering greater rewards and tougher opponents:

Elite Officers: Face legendary characters with unique weapons and abilities. These battles demand precision and strategy.

Heroic Trials: Special skirmishes that limit player abilities or impose strict conditions, such as reduced health or restricted weapon types. Faction-Specific Skirmishes: Aligning with certain factions unlocks exclusive missions that explore their storylines and provide faction-themed rewards.

6. Tips for Maximizing Rewards

Replay for Perfection: Use Free Mode to revisit skirmishes and improve your rank, unlocking better rewards.

Focus on Secondary Objectives: Completing these can yield additional experience points and rare items.

Experiment with Characters: Try different heroes and companions in skirmishes to find new strategies and playstyles.

Visiting Towns and Interacting with NPCs

Towns in Dynasty Warriors: Origins serve as vital hubs for players to rest, regroup, and engage with the world beyond the battlefield. NPCs provide a wealth of opportunities, including quests, trades, and lore, enriching the player's experience in the Three Kingdoms era. This subchapter explores the functionality of towns, the role of NPCs, and how to make the most of these interactions.

1. The Role of Towns in the Game
Towns are scattered throughout the game world and offer various services and activities that enhance both gameplay and immersion.

Rest and Resupply:
Players can heal, replenish consumables, and repair equipment.
Inns and taverns provide a place to restore health and stamina.

Trade and Commerce:
Merchants sell weapons, armor, and rare crafting materials.
Blacksmiths offer weapon upgrades, customizations, and crafting services.

Quest Hubs:

Many side quests originate from NPCs in towns, offering rewards like rare items and experience points.

2. NPC Types and Their Roles

Towns are populated by a diverse range of NPCs, each with specific roles and benefits for the player:

Merchants:
Function: Sell and trade items such as weapons, consumables, and crafting materials.
Tip: Check merchants' inventories regularly, as stock updates with story progression or after completing missions.

Blacksmiths:
Function: Upgrade, repair, and customize weapons. Some blacksmiths specialize in crafting rare items using unique blueprints.
Tip: Invest in blacksmith services to unlock advanced weapon options and discounts.

Quest Givers:
Function: Offer side missions or special tasks. Some quests are tied to specific NPCs and their story arcs.
Tip: Engage with all quest-giving NPCs to discover hidden missions or lore.

Trainers:
Function: Provide combat tutorials and skill enhancement opportunities.
Tip: Use trainers to refine your skills and unlock advanced combat techniques.

Civilians and Informants:
Function: Provide lore, rumors, and tips about hidden treasures or upcoming challenges.
Tip: Talking to informants can reveal optional missions or shortcuts to rare rewards.

3. Interactions and Their Benefits

Interacting with NPCs in towns often leads to valuable gameplay opportunities:

Dialogue Choices:
Some NPC interactions include dialogue options that can affect affinity levels, unlock quests, or provide strategic advantages.
Example: Choosing to assist a struggling villager might lead to a quest with a rare weapon reward.

Trading Materials:
Certain NPCs specialize in bartering, allowing players to exchange excess resources for rare items.

Building Relationships:
Regular interactions with key NPCs can unlock additional services or discounts.

4. Unique Town Events

Towns are more than static hubs; they often host dynamic events that provide unique rewards:

Festivals and Celebrations:
Special events in towns can grant bonuses, such as increased experience gain or discounts at shops.
 Example: A harvest festival might offer rare food items that temporarily boost your character's stats.

Enemy Raids:
Some towns are subject to surprise attacks, triggering optional defense missions. Successfully defending the town earns rewards and strengthens relationships with its inhabitants.

Faction Influence:
The allegiance of a town may shift based on your decisions in the campaign. Aligning with a faction can unlock exclusive services or quests.

5. Exploring Town Features

Hidden Secrets:
Search alleys, rooftops, or behind buildings for hidden chests, collectibles, or lore items.
Tip: Use companions with scouting abilities to locate hard-to-find secrets.

Mini-Games:
Some towns feature mini-games like archery contests or dueling arenas, providing additional ways to earn rewards.

Customization Options:
Visit tailors or artisans to customize your character's appearance, adding a personal touch to your journey.

6. Tips for Efficient Town Visits
Plan Ahead: Make a checklist of items to buy, quests to accept, and upgrades to complete before leaving a town.
Check Regularly: Revisit towns after major story events to discover new quests, stock, or NPCs.
Balance Resources: Prioritize spending currency and materials on essential upgrades before luxury items.

Unlockable Content and Secrets

Dynasty Warriors: Origins is filled with hidden treasures, secret missions, and unlockable content that add depth and replayability to the game. Discovering these secrets often requires exploration, puzzle-solving, or achieving specific milestones. This subchapter guides players through the types of unlockable content available, where to find them, and how to access the game's most rewarding secrets.

1. Types of Unlockable Content
The game offers a variety of hidden content to reward players for their dedication:

Hidden Characters:
Legendary figures from the Three Kingdoms era that are not part of the main roster.
Examples: Unlock characters like Zhou Tai or Xu Shu by completing special missions or meeting specific conditions.

Exclusive Weapons and Gear:
Rare and unique weapons with distinct abilities and appearances.
Found in hidden chests, rewarded for completing secret objectives, or earned through challenging skirmishes.

Alternate Outfits and Skins:

Unlock aesthetic options for your characters, such as historically inspired outfits or themed skins.
Often tied to completing faction-specific storylines or achievements.

Secret Missions and Campaigns:
Hidden missions that provide unique challenges or reveal untold stories.
Completing these missions often grants significant rewards, including rare items or new endings.

Achievements and Titles:
Completing difficult tasks unlocks achievements or in-game titles that showcase your accomplishments.

2. How to Unlock Hidden Content
Accessing unlockable content requires exploration, combat expertise, and attention to detail:

Exploration and Discovery:
Search all areas of the map, including off-the-beaten-path locations, for hidden treasure chests or NPCs offering secret quests. Use companions with scouting abilities to uncover concealed objectives.

Meeting Specific Conditions:

Some unlockables require achieving certain feats, such as defeating a boss without taking damage or completing a mission within a time limit.
Example: To unlock a secret mission, finish three related skirmishes with an S rank.

Choices and Branching Paths:
Decisions made during the campaign can unlock or block access to certain content.
Example: Aligning with a particular faction may open exclusive missions or characters while locking others.

Achievement-Based Rewards:
Achieving high ranks in missions or completing optional objectives can unlock content.
Example: Achieve S rank in all missions of a campaign to unlock a legendary weapon.

3. Notable Hidden Secrets
The game includes some standout hidden content worth pursuing:

The "Mystic Artifacts" Side Quest:
Discover and collect ancient artifacts scattered across the map to unlock a secret character with mystical abilities.

Zhuge Liang's Alternate Storyline:

Fulfill specific objectives in the Shu campaign to unlock an alternate storyline that explores his hidden strategies and alliances.

The Forbidden Armory:
Accessible only after completing the campaign on the highest difficulty, this location contains some of the most powerful weapons in the game.

Hidden Dialogue and Lore:
Engage with NPCs and complete their personal quests to uncover detailed lore about the Three Kingdoms and gain new insights into the characters.

4. Tips for Uncovering Secrets
Replay Missions: Use Free Mode to revisit earlier missions and explore areas you may have missed.
Interact with All NPCs: NPCs often drop hints about hidden content or offer quests that lead to unlockables.
Analyze the Map: Look for unexplored regions or areas marked with question marks, indicating hidden opportunities.
Experiment with Choices: Try different dialogue options or alignments to access alternate paths and content.
Complete Optional Challenges: Many secrets are tied to bonus objectives or specific feats achieved during missions.

5. The Rewards of Unlocking Secrets

Discovering hidden content not only provides tangible rewards like weapons and characters but also enriches the overall gameplay experience:
Replayability: Unlocked content encourages multiple playthroughs to explore all the game's possibilities.
Personalization: Rare outfits, weapons, and abilities allow players to customize their journey.
Lore and Story Depth: Hidden missions and dialogue add layers to the narrative, deepening your connection to the world of the Three Kingdoms.

Chapter 8: Tips and Strategies

Combat Tips for Beginners and Advanced Players

Mastering the combat system in Dynasty Warriors: Origins is key to dominating the battlefield. Whether you're a new player or a seasoned veteran, refining your techniques and learning advanced strategies can enhance your experience. This subchapter covers essential combat tips for players at all levels.

1. Beginner Tips: Starting Strong

Learn Basic Combos:
Experiment with light and heavy attack combinations to discover effective moves.
Most characters have unique combos that can be chained for crowd control or single-target damage.

Master the Stamina System:
Keep an eye on your stamina bar, as it governs actions like dodging, parrying, and executing special moves.
Avoid overusing stamina-intensive actions to prevent vulnerability.

Stay Mobile:

Movement is critical in combat. Use dashes and jumps to evade attacks and reposition yourself against enemies.

Target Key Enemies:
Focus on eliminating enemy officers and commanders first, as their defeat often weakens the morale of surrounding troops.
Use Environmental Elements: Take advantage of destructible objects, chokepoints, and traps to gain an edge in battles.

2. Intermediate Tips: Refining Your Skills
Utilize Character Arts:
Each character's unique Art can turn the tide of battle. Time these abilities carefully to maximize their impact.

Parry and Counter:
Perfecting your parry timing allows you to stagger enemies and launch devastating counterattacks.
Use counters to break through heavily armored foes or disrupt enemy officers.
Switch Between Weapons: Many characters can equip multiple weapons. Switching during combat can maintain combo flow or exploit enemy weaknesses.

Manage Companion Roles:

Assign companions to support, defend, or attack based on your current objectives. Their abilities can complement your strategy.

3. Advanced Tips: Mastering the Battlefield

Maximize Combos:
Advanced players can chain combos across groups of enemies, maintaining a high combo multiplier for increased damage and rewards.
Experiment with timing and directional inputs to unlock hidden combo variations.

Exploit Enemy Weaknesses:
Study enemy types to identify weaknesses. Use weapons with traits or elemental effects that counter specific foes.

Leverage Morale Mechanics:
Boost your troops' morale by completing objectives and defeating key enemies. High morale increases allied effectiveness and makes battles easier.

Control the Battlefield:
Focus on capturing strategic points like strongholds and supply depots. Controlling the battlefield reduces enemy reinforcements and grants tactical advantages.

4. Common Mistakes to Avoid

Ignoring Defense: Neglecting parries, blocks, or evasions often leads to unnecessary damage. Balance offense with defensive strategies.

Overcommitting to Combos: Long combos leave you vulnerable to counterattacks. Always remain aware of your surroundings and retreat if necessary.

Neglecting Companions:
Underutilized companions can hinder your effectiveness. Assign them roles and make use of their abilities.

5. Advanced Challenges

Elite Enemies and Boss Fights:
Focus on precision and patience when facing powerful enemies like Lü Bu. Learn their attack patterns and capitalize on openings.
Use ranged attacks or elemental weapons to exploit their weaknesses.

High-Difficulty Modes:
In higher difficulty settings, enemies hit harder and have higher health. Use refined strategies, upgraded weapons, and companion abilities to succeed.

6. Tips for Improving Over Time**

Practice in Free Mode:
Revisit previous missions to practice combos, experiment with weapons, and refine your skills.

Study the Map:
Familiarize yourself with battlefield layouts to plan your strategy effectively.

Adapt to Your Playstyle:
While general tips are helpful, focus on mastering characters and strategies that align with your preferred playstyle.

Effective Use of Tactics and Companions

In Dynasty Warriors: Origins, success on the battlefield often hinges on how effectively you deploy tactics and leverage your companions' unique abilities. Mastering these elements allows players to control the flow of battle, overcome challenges, and maximize their strategic potential. This subchapter explores key tactical concepts and provides actionable strategies for utilizing companions in a variety of scenarios.

1. Understanding Tactics

Tactics are the backbone of battlefield success, enabling players to adapt to dynamic situations and outmaneuver opponents.

Pre-Battle Planning:
Review the mission objectives and enemy layout on the map before engaging.
Equip weapons, traits, and companions suited to the mission type.

Focus on Objectives:
Prioritize mission-critical goals over engaging every enemy. Completing objectives efficiently often reduces overall resistance.

Control Strategic Points:
Capture strongholds, supply depots, and outposts to weaken enemy forces and bolster allied morale.
Stronghold control also reduces enemy reinforcements and provides safe zones for regrouping.

Flanking and Ambushes:
Use the map to identify routes for flanking enemy positions.
Set up ambushes with companions to disrupt enemy formations and morale.

Adaptive Strategies:

Be prepared to switch tactics mid-battle if the situation changes, such as reinforcements arriving or a high-value target appearing.

2. Companion Roles and Deployment
Companions provide critical support in battle, each offering unique abilities and roles that complement the player's strategy.

Assigning Roles:
Offensive Role: Assign aggressive companions to take down high-priority targets or push through enemy lines. Defensive Role: Place defensive companions at chokepoints or near objectives to hold the line.
Support Role: Deploy supportive companions to buff allies, heal troops, or disrupt enemy formations.

Commanding Companions:
Use the command wheel to assign specific tasks, such as attacking a target, defending a location, or regrouping with the player. Monitor their status during battle and adjust commands as needed.

3. Maximizing Companion Abilities
Each companion has unique abilities that can turn the tide of battle when used effectively.

Active Skills:

Time these abilities for maximum impact, such as using an AoE skill to break a crowd or a stun ability to neutralize an enemy officer.

Combo Attacks:

Build affinity with companions to unlock powerful synchronized attacks. These moves deal significant damage and often have area-of-effect capabilities.

Passive Traits:

Choose companions whose passive traits align with your strategy, such as increased morale, faster resource gathering, or improved stamina regeneration.

4. Tactical Coordination

Effective teamwork between the player and companions is essential for success in larger battles.

Divide and Conquer:

Assign companions to handle secondary objectives or enemy clusters while you focus on the main task.

Overwhelming Force:

Concentrate your team's efforts on key enemy officers or strongholds to quickly gain control of the battlefield.

Dual Engagements:

Use one companion to distract or pin down enemies while another supports your direct assault.

5. Leveraging Companions in Specific Scenarios

Defensive Missions:
Assign companions with high defensive stats to hold key positions while you patrol the battlefield.
Escort Missions: Use supportive companions to heal or protect NPCs while assigning an offensive ally to clear the path.
Siege Battles:
Deploy companions to attack siege equipment or protect engineers working on battering rams.

6. Improving Companion Effectiveness

Build Affinity:
Strengthen relationships with companions by completing missions together, engaging in dialogue, and fulfilling their requests. High affinity unlocks enhanced abilities and personal missions.
Upgrade Their Equipment: Equip companions with weapons and gear that complement their role. Upgrading their equipment ensures they remain effective in high-difficulty missions.
Train Companions:
Visit trainers or engage in camp activities to improve their skills and unlock new abilities.

7. Tips for Balancing Tactics and Companions

Adapt to the Mission: Tailor your strategy and companion deployment to the specific objectives and challenges of each mission.

Utilize the Mini-Map: Monitor companion positions and enemy movements to adjust your tactics dynamically.

Experiment with Pairings: Test different companion combinations to find synergies that suit your playstyle.

Managing Resources and Upgrades

Effective resource management and strategic upgrades are essential for thriving in Dynasty Warriors: Origins. From maintaining a strong economy to ensuring your equipment and abilities are up to par, this subchapter offers a detailed guide on optimizing resources and upgrades for sustained success.

1. Types of Resources and Their Uses

The game features several key resources, each with specific applications:

Currency:

Used to purchase weapons, consumables, and crafting materials.

Earned through completing missions, defeating enemies, and trading items.

Crafting Materials:
Essential for upgrading weapons, creating custom gear, and refining traits.
Found by looting treasure chests, completing side quests, or harvesting resource nodes.

Skill Points:
Earned through leveling up and completing challenges, skill points unlock and upgrade character abilities.

Energy or Stamina Items:
Consumables like potions or food restore health, stamina, or provide temporary buffs.
Acquired from merchants, treasure chests, or crafted with specific recipes.

2. Prioritizing Resource Allocation
Early Game:
Focus on upgrading essential weapons and acquiring basic consumables.
Avoid overspending on cosmetic items or non-essential upgrades.
Mid to Late Game:
Invest in refining rare weapons and crafting advanced gear.
Prioritize unlocking high-level abilities and traits that align with your playstyle.

Emergency Reserves:
Always maintain a stock of essential consumables and currency for unexpected challenges, such as boss battles or difficult missions.

3. Efficient Resource Gathering
Complete Side Missions:
Side missions often yield high rewards, including currency, crafting materials, and rare items.
Explore Thoroughly: Search every battlefield for treasure chests, resource nodes, and hidden caches.
Target High-Value Enemies:
Elite officers and bosses often drop rare items and large sums of currency.
Trading and Bartering:
Engage with merchants and bartering NPCs to acquire rare materials or trade excess items.

4. Weapon and Equipment Upgrades
Upgrade Regularly:
Ensure your weapons remain competitive by upgrading them with materials and currency.
Focus on traits and attributes that enhance your combat effectiveness.
Refine and Customize:
 Use the refinement system to modify weapons and add traits that suit upcoming challenges.

Example: Equip fire traits for battles against large enemy groups or ice traits for slowing down fast opponents.
Craft Unique Weapons:
Collect blueprints and materials to create custom weapons with specialized effects.

5. Skill Tree and Ability Management
Unlock Core Abilities First:
Focus on abilities that enhance your primary combat style or provide essential buffs.
Specialize Your Playstyle: Invest skill points in traits that complement your preferred strategy, such as offensive, defensive, or support roles.
Upgrade Companion Abilities:
Don't neglect companions—enhance their skills to ensure they remain effective partners in battle.

6. Tips for Managing Consumables

Stock Up Before Missions:
Visit merchants or supply points to replenish health potions, stamina restorers, and buff items.
Use Consumables Strategically:
Save powerful consumables for critical moments, such as boss fights or difficult objectives.

7. Long-Term Upgrade Strategies

Plan for Future Challenges: Analyze upcoming missions to determine which upgrades will provide the greatest advantage.

Rotate Equipment:

Regularly switch between weapons and gear to keep all options viable.

Maximize Affinity Rewards:

High-affinity companions often provide unique upgrades or items, so invest in building relationships.

8. Avoiding Common Mistakes

Over-Upgrading Early Gear:

Avoid maxing out low-tier weapons—save resources for higher-quality equipment.

Neglecting Resource Nodes:

Always gather from resource points, even if they seem insignificant initially.

9. Resource Management in High-Difficulty Modes

Prioritize Survival:

Focus on upgrading defensive gear and traits to withstand tougher enemies.

Optimize Efficiency:

Use consumables sparingly and rely on tactics and companion abilities to conserve resources.

Achievements and Trophies Guide

Achievements and trophies in Dynasty Warriors: Origins provide players with goals that enhance gameplay, encourage exploration, and reward mastery of the game's mechanics. From story milestones to skill-based challenges, completing these tasks is both satisfying and rewarding. This subchapter outlines the categories of achievements, tips for earning them, and their significance.

1. Categories of Achievements and Trophies

Achievements are grouped into categories that align with different aspects of gameplay:
Story-Based Achievements: Earned by progressing through the main campaign and completing key chapters. Examples: "The Yellow Turban Rebellion" – Complete Chapter 1. "Victory at Chibi" – Defeat Cao Cao's fleet in the Battle of Chibi.

Combat Achievements:
Awarded for demonstrating skill and mastery in battle.
Examples: "Combo King" – Achieve a 500-hit combo. "Untouchable" – Complete a mission without taking damage.

Exploration Achievements:

Reward players for discovering hidden areas, secrets, and treasures.
 Examples:
"Treasure Hunter" – Find 50 hidden chests.
"Map Master" – Fully explore every battlefield.

Progression Achievements:
Recognize milestones in leveling up, upgrading, or resource gathering.
Examples:
"Master Craftsman" – Fully upgrade 10 weapons. "Elite Commander" – Reach level 50 with any character.

Relationship Achievements: Focused on building bonds with companions and completing their storylines.
Examples: "Trusted Ally" – Max out affinity with 5 companions.
"Heart of the Three Kingdoms" – Unlock all companion-specific quests.

Challenge Achievements:
Reserved for completing difficult tasks or optional content.
Examples: "Conqueror of Chaos" – Complete the campaign on the hardest difficulty.
"Skirmish Master" – Earn an S rank in 20 skirmishes.

2. Tips for Earning Achievements and Trophies

Plan Ahead:
Review the achievement list early to identify objectives that can be completed during regular gameplay.
Focus on multi-objective missions that contribute to multiple achievements.

Replay Missions:
Use Free Mode to revisit missions and improve your performance, especially for time-based or rank-dependent achievements.

Practice Combat Mastery:
Achievements tied to combos, perfect dodges, or parries often require practice. Experiment with different characters and weapons to find your strengths.

Explore Thoroughly:
Many achievements are tied to discovering hidden content. Search every battlefield and town for secrets.

Build Relationships:
Engage with companions consistently to unlock their quests and achieve affinity-related goals.

3. High-Difficulty Achievements

Preparation Is Key:
Upgrade your weapons, refine traits, and enhance companion abilities before tackling high-difficulty challenges.
Focus on Survival:
Defensive playstyles, healing consumables, and supportive companions are essential for harder missions.
Study Enemy Patterns:
Learn the attack patterns of elite officers and bosses to maximize your chances of success.

4. Achievement Tracking and Progress
In-Game Tracking:
Use the achievements menu to monitor your progress and identify goals you're close to completing.
Incremental Goals:
Break down larger achievements into smaller, manageable tasks to make steady progress.

5. Notable Achievement Rewards

Completing certain achievements unlocks in-game bonuses:

Exclusive Items: Rare weapons, outfits, and crafting materials.

Titles and Badges: Showcase your accomplishments in multiplayer or co-op modes.
Hidden Content: Achievements tied to exploration or storylines often reveal additional lore or missions.

6. Common Pitfalls to Avoid
Ignoring Missable Achievements:
Some achievements are tied to specific missions or choices. Check requirements before progressing too far in the story.
Overlooking Side Missions:
Many achievements require side quest completion, so engage with optional content regularly.
Focusing Solely on the Main Campaign:
Balance your time between campaign progress and optional objectives to maximize achievement opportunities.

7. Benefits of Pursuing Achievements

Replayability: Encourages players to revisit missions and explore alternate strategies.
Skill Development: Many achievements require mastery of combat and tactics, improving overall gameplay.
Satisfaction and Completion: Completing the full achievement list is a rewarding way to experience everything the game has to offer.

www.ingramcontent.com/pod-product-compliance
Lightning Source LLC
Chambersburg PA
CBHW071057240526
45471CB00016B/1979